(God's Plan 4 You)

by Kara Eckmann Powell

Gospel Light is an evangelical Christian publisher dedicated to serving the local church. We believe God's vision for Gospel Light is to provide church leaders with biblical, user-friendly materials that will help them evangelize, disciple and minister to children, youth and families.

We hope this Gospel Light resource will help you discover biblical truth for your own life and help you minister to youth. God bless you in your work.

For a free catalog of resources from Gospel Light please contact your Christian supplier or contact us at 1-800-4-GOSPEL.

PUBLISHING STAFF

William T. Greig, Publisher
Dr. Elmer L. Towns, Senior Consulting Publisher
Dr. Gary S. Greig, Senior Consulting Editor
Pam Weston, Editor
Patti Pennington Virtue, Assistant Editor
Christi Goeser, Editorial Assistant
Kyle Duncan, Associate Publisher
Bayard Taylor, M.Div., Senior Editor, Theological and Biblical Issues
Kevin Parks, Cover Designer
Debi Thayer, Designer

ISBN 0-8307-2406-0
© 1999 by Gospel Light
All rights reserved.
Printed in U.S.A.

All Scripture quotations, unless otherwise indicated, are taken from the *Holy Bible, New International Version®. NIV®.* Copyright © 1973, 1978, 1984 by International Bible Society. Used by permission of Zondervan Publishing House. All rights reserved.
Other version used is:
MESSAGE—Scripture taken from *THE MESSAGE*. Copyright © by Eugene H. Peterson, 1993, 1994, 1995. Used by permission of NavPress Publishing Group.

How to Make Clean Copies from This Book

You may make copies of portions of this book with a clean conscience if:

- you (or someone in your organization) are the original purchaser;
- you are using the copies you make for a noncommercial purpose (such as teaching or promoting your ministry) within your church or organization;
- you follow the instructions provided in this book.

However, it is illegal for you to make copies if:

- you are using the material to promote, advertise or sell a product or service other than for ministry fund-raising;
- you are using the material in or on a product for sale;
- you or your organization are **not** the original purchaser of this book.

By following these guidelines you help us keep our products affordable.
Thank you,
Gospel Light

Permission to make photocopies or to reproduce by any other mechanical or electronic means in whole or in part of any designated* page, illustration or activity in this book is granted only to the original purchaser and is intended for noncommercial use within a church or other Christian organization. None of the material in this book may be reproduced for any commercial promotion, advertising or sale of a product or service. Sharing of the material in this book with other churches or organizations not owned or controlled by the original purchaser is also prohibited. All rights reserved.

*Pages with the following notation can be legally reproduced:
© 1999 by Gospel Light. Permission to photocopy granted. *GP4U (God's Plan for You)*

Contents

How to Use **GP4U**		7
Introducing Young People to Christ		9
Session One:	**Perfection in His Eyes**	11
	The God who made the universe created you and loves you as you are.	
Session Two:	**Our Only Roadblock**	25
	Sin separates us from God.	
Session Three:	**One Way Only**	37
	God's son, Jesus, gives us a clear picture of what God is like.	
Session Four:	**Jesus Paid the Price**	51
	We can receive forgiveness for our sins and new life because of Jesus' death and resurrection.	
Session Five:	**Ambassadors for His Kingdom**	63
	You can live as God's child and show His love to others.	
Bonus Section:	**How Can I Get to Know Jesus?**	77

How to Use GP4U

This 5- to 10-session course is designed to help junior high students discover God's awesome love.

During this course students will discover or review that…
- The same God who made the universe created us and loves us as we are;
- Sin blocks us from receiving God's love;
- Jesus Christ is our "picture" of God;
- Jesus made it possible for us to receive forgiveness and to be in God's family;
- We can live as God's children and show His love to others.

You can use *GP4U* for Vacation Bible School, camp or retreat—or your regular youth fellowship meetings any time of the year. *GP4U* is designed to be a flexible course with the ability to expand from 5 to 10 sessions.

About Involvement Learning

So often we hear or read accounts of youth who live empty lives and have no apparent goals or direction in life. To fill the emptiness, they often turn to activities that ultimately only heighten that emptiness. Now more than ever, today's youth need to know that the potential to live this dynamic kind of life is firmly rooted in the study of and obedience to God's Word.

It takes courage to live an obedient life and it takes strength to overcome the many barriers to Christian growth erected by the world. Therefore, it is not enough to simply tell today's youth that studying and obeying God's Word will lead to a productive life. Many teachers have helped their youth know this truth for themselves through involvement learning.

The teaching methods and materials in this book emphasize involvement learning. These methods will involve your students in the learning process and take them from the role of passively listening to one of actively digging into the Scriptures. These methods will help you create in your students the desire to examine God's Word and to make practical applications of the truths being studied.

Each session in this study includes three activities for each session:
- **Approach the Word**—involves students in activities that capture and direct their interest toward the theme of the session.
- **Bible Exploration**—students use a variety of methods to learn what the Bible says about the session's theme.
- **Conclusion and Decision**—involves each student in a discussion or activity that provides a way to apply the Bible truths to his or her own life.

Within each session is an option to expand the session to two meetings, making a total of 10 sessions. If you are using the five-session track, the following note gives you the directions at the end of the Bible Exploration:

> **Note:** If you are completing this session in one meeting, skip to "Conclusion and Decision."

Immediately following this note you will find directions for expanding to a 10-session study:

> **Two-Meeting Track:** If you want to spread this session over two meetings, STOP here and close in prayer. Inform students of the content to be covered in your next meeting.

The **Two-Meeting Track** box is then followed by:
- **Review and Approach**—gives an opportunity for review of the previous lesson and an introduction to the Bible Exploration Two;
- **Bible Exploration Two**—further expands on the Bible study of the previous session.

The ideas provided in these sessions may stimulate additional ideas of your own that fit your group and teaching style. It is our prayer that the learning experiences suggested in this book, coupled with the power of God's Word, will challenge and motivate your students—encouraging some to become Christians and stirring up those who have grown complacent in their spiritual lives.

Introducing Young People to Christ

How do you present Christ to a young person?
1. **Pray.** Ask God to prepare the hearts of students to receive the message and prepare you to present it.
2. **Lay the foundation.** Youth are evaluating you and the Lord you serve by everything you do and say. They are looking for people in whose lives knowing God makes a noticeable difference, for people who love them and listen to them—the same way God loves them and listens to them.

    Learn to listen with your full attention. Learn to share honestly both the joys and the struggles you encounter as a Christian. Be honest about your own questions and about your personal concern for students. Learn to accept teens as they are. Christ died for them while they were yet sinners. You are also called to love them as they are.
3. **Be aware of opportunities.** A student may ask to talk after class. Or some might be waiting for you to suggest going for a soda—getting alone together where you can share what Jesus Christ means to you.
4. **Have a plan.** Don't lecture or force the issue. Here are some tips to keep in mind:
    - **Put the student at ease.** Be perceptive of feelings and remember he or she is probably nervous. Be relaxed, natural and casual in your conversation, not critical or judgmental.
    - **Get the student to talk**, and listen carefully to what is said. Students sometimes make superficial or shocking statements just to get your reaction. Don't begin lecturing or problem solving. Instead encourage him or her to keep talking.
    - **Be gently direct.** Students may have trouble bringing up the topic. If you sense this, a simple question like, "How are you and God getting along?" can unlock a life-changing conversation.
    - **Discuss God's desire to have fellowship with people.** As you relate the plan God has for enabling people to have a relationship with Him, move through the points slowly enough to allow time for thinking and comprehending. However, do not drag out the presentation:
        a. God's goal for us is abundant life (see John 3:16; 10:10).
        b. All people are separated from God by sin (see Romans 3:23; 6:23).
        c. God's solution is Jesus Christ who died to pay the penalty for our sin (see John 14:6; Romans 5:8).
        d. Our response is to receive Christ as Savior (see John 1:12).
    - **Make sure the student understands that accepting Christ is very simple,** though very profound. If you feel the student understands, ask if he or she would like to accept Christ now. If so, ask the student to pray with you. Explain that praying is simply talking to God. In this case it's telling God of the student's need for Christ and desire for Christ to be in his or her life as personal Lord and Savior. Then suggest that the student study in order to begin growing in the faith.

        If the student feels unready to make a decision, suggest some Scripture to read and make an appointment to get together again. John 14—16; Romans 3—8 and the Gospel of Mark are good sections of Scripture for reading. Pray for the student in the meantime.
5. **Remember your responsibility is simply to present the gospel** and to be able to explain the hope that is within you. It is the Holy Spirit who makes the heart ready for a relationship with God and gives growth.

When It's All Said and Done

When it's all said and done, what is done will far outlast what is said.

The time you invest in building relationships, encouraging and affirming students, listening to them and putting up with their rowdy moods (which seem to be never ending) will pay dividends in the kingdom of God.

It is the personal touch that does it. Kids know when someone cares for them. It shows. It pays off. It declares loudly, "Here is a real person who has a real relationship with Christ, who wants to know the real you."

Relationships should not end with the packing away of materials. New contacts have been made during these days. These contacts need to be followed up.

Plan follow-up for those who become Christians. Get them into Sunday School. Visit their homes to answer questions and give encouragement. Provide transportation when needed.

Plan follow-up for those who rededicate their lives to the Lord. They need guidance in Bible study, in prayer and in preparing for the work the Lord has for them.

Plan follow-up for the unsaved. Invite them to church youth activities. Bring them to Sunday School and worship services. Continue to pray for them by name and keep in touch with them. Remember birthdays with a card or phone call.

Plan follow-up for unchurched parents. Show genuine interest in their young people. Continue to invite the entire family to church services and church activities—especially to adult Bible classes.

And when that once ornery student begins to respond to the love and caring you have shown, don't be surprised if he or she thinks about you and what you did to demonstrate God's love—and then tries to do the same for someone else.

SESSION 1

Perfection in His Eyes

Leader's Devotional

A group of psychologists conducting some pioneering research decided to investigate the relationship between an adult's physical appearance and his or her social interaction. They brought several adults (a.k.a. human-sized guinea pigs) into individual mirrorless rooms and explained to each that they were going to use makeup to create a scar on his or her face. A talented makeup artist then used creative makeup techniques to add a large and noticeable scar to each person's face, one at a time in the individual rooms.

In each instance, after the makeup artist finished applying the scar, he held up a mirror so that the subject could see what he had done. The makeup artist then removed the mirror and told the subject that he was going to dab some "finishing powder" onto the scar so that the scar wouldn't smear. In reality, he wiped away the scar, leaving the subject's face unblemished. Although the subjects thought they had a new scar, in reality their appearance was unaltered.

Each volunteer was then sent into a new social setting, such as a doctor's office or a car mechanic's waiting room to observe and record how people interacted with him or her. Without exception, the subjects returned and made the following kinds of comments:

"People were more rude to me."
"People were mean to me."
"People stared at my scar."

This true story captures the emotions of every junior higher who sits before you during this session. They feel scarred. For some it may be a physical imperfection, such as acne or a seemingly endless succession of bad hair days that leaves them convinced that the whole world is staring at them. For others it may be areas of insecurity, such as difficulty making friends or fear of being "different" from anyone else that leaves them feeling exposed and vulnerable.

No matter what it is that makes him or her feel insecure, every junior higher feels inadequate. That's why this session is such good news for the confused and unsure students in your ministry—which is *all* of them! The God who made the universe created them. More than that, He loves them. He has made them each a perfect 10. *No one* is imperfect; we are all molded to perfection. And what a privilege you have to bring this transforming truth to junior highers!

Session 1 Perfection in His Eyes

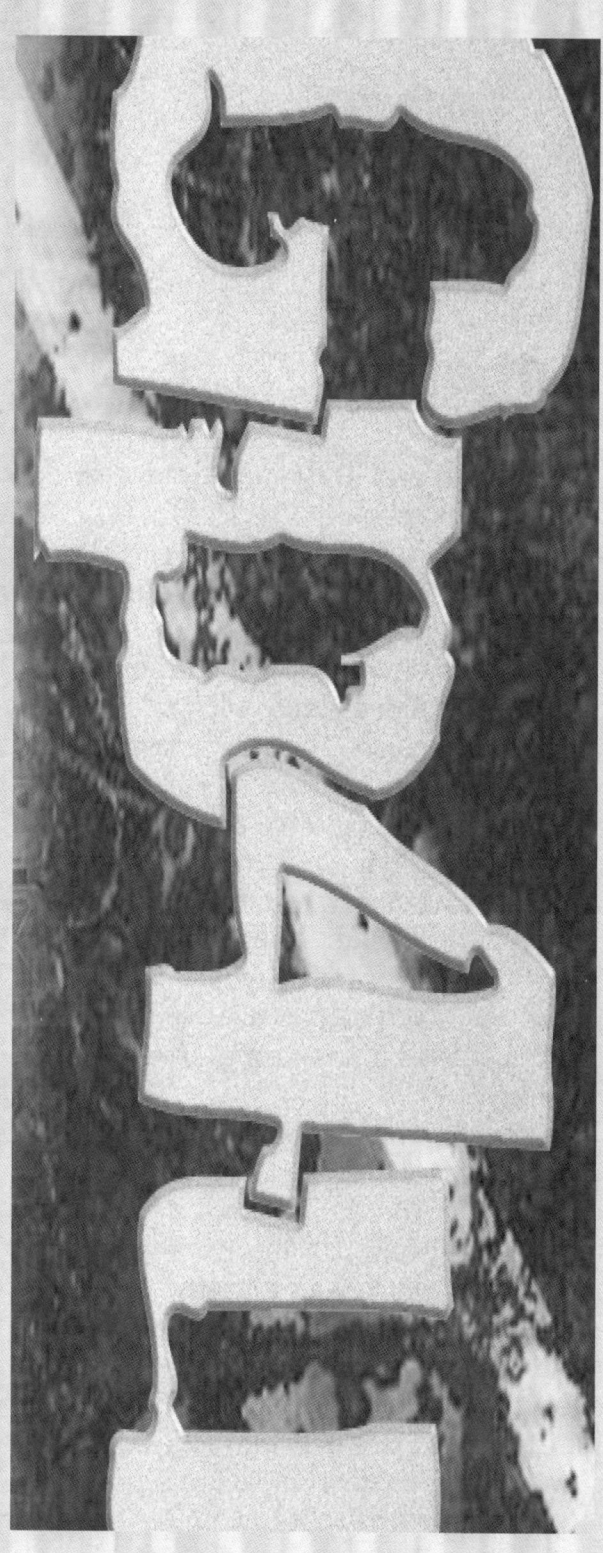

Key Verse

"God saw all that he had made, and it was very good." Genesis 1:31

Biblical Basis

Genesis 1:1—2:3; Psalm 138:8; 139:14

Focus of This Session

The God who made the universe created you and loves you as you are.

Aims of This Session

During this session students will:
- Discover that God's creation is good and perfect;
- Feel comforted and secure knowing that the Creator God made them absolutely unique and loves them just as they are;
- Act by choosing words that describe how God feels about them.

Approach the Word

15 MINUTES

OBJECTIVE
To help students understand that only God can make something new out of nothing.

MATERIALS AND PREPARATION NEEDED
- Balloons, at least one for each student and one extra
- Yarn or string, cut in 18- to 24-inch pieces, one for each student
- Baking soda
- Vinegar

Ahead of time, practice the balloon, baking soda and vinegar trick described below, using *small* amounts of each because the balloon could burst and you don't want vinegar or balloon pieces hitting your eye.

Greet students and explain that you're starting this new series with a game. Have them remove their shoes. Give each student a balloon to blow up and tie. Next, give a piece of yarn to each student and have them tie their balloons to one of their ankles. Explain that when you say go, students should try to stomp others' balloons while protecting their own from attack.

When a student's balloon is popped, he or she is eliminated. You might want to have extra balloons and strings so students can return to the game until all the extra balloons are gone.

Option: To make it even more fun, divide students into two teams (such as the old standby, boys against girls, or seventh graders against eighth graders). Give each team one color of balloons (for example, one team has red balloons and one team has blue ones); then have them try to pop the balloons of the other team. Congratulate the student who is the last one to have a balloon still intact on his or her ankle.

After everyone is seated, explain that you're going to do another trick with a balloon. Pour a *small* amount of baking soda into a balloon, then pour in some vinegar and tie the balloon. The balloon will swell up with carbon dioxide. Explain: **Making a balloon swell up is a pretty neat trick, but it didn't happen on its own. We needed a balloon, some baking soda and vinegar. We can never make** something out of nothing. There's only one Person who can do that—God. Only *He* can make something out of nothing, and He did just that to create the earth and to create us. Today we're going to look closer at what that means.

Bible Exploration One

30 MINUTES

OBJECTIVE
To help students understand that God says His creation is good and that our purpose is to worship Him.

MATERIALS AND PREPARATION NEEDED
- ❏ Several Bibles
- ❏ One copy of "Word Up" (p. 21), cut into six individual cards
- ❏ A bag of small, individually wrapped candies for prizes

For this activity, you'll need 6 to 12 student volunteers (it doesn't matter if that's your whole group or if it's just a portion of your group), divided into two teams by either grade or gender.

Select a contestant from each team to begin the game and show them both the first card with four words on it. Be sure to tell them not to say the words out loud. Instruct each contestant to bid on the number of word *clues* that he or she thinks it will take for his or her team to guess all four words on the card. The lowest bid wins the chance to play first. If all four words on the card are guessed, using the number of word clues bid or less, the team earns two points. If the number of clues is exceeded, the team loses three points. Repeat the whole process using new volunteers for each of the six word cards. At the end of the game, the team with the most points wins.

After the game is completed, ask for a volunteer to read Genesis 1:1—2:3. As the volunteer is reading, instruct students to stand up if they hear any of the words read that were on the cards. Throw a piece of candy to everyone who recognizes a word and stands. This will keep students listening attentively to the details of God's creation.

Read the Scripture one more time, asking students to listen for any words that appear more than *three* times. Explain:

Outside of the obvious words of "the" and "and," two of the words that appear the most are "God" and "good."

Discuss:

How do the words "God" and "good" fit together—besides the fact that they have the same letters? Everything God creates is good because He *is* good.

How does the word "said" relate to the words "good" and "God"? God is so powerful that He speaks and stuff happens.

Is there anything God created that isn't good? No, it's all good because He made it.

Since it's good, how should we act toward creation? Realizing it is a gift from God to us, we should treat His creation with respect.

Since God made the heavens, the earth and everything in them, including each of us, what should our response be? We should worship Him, thank Him, love Him, etc.!

> **Note:** If you are completing this session in one meeting, skip to "Conclusion and Decision."

> **Two-Meeting Track:** If you want to spread this session over two meetings, STOP here and close in prayer. Inform students of the content to be covered in your next meeting.

NOTES

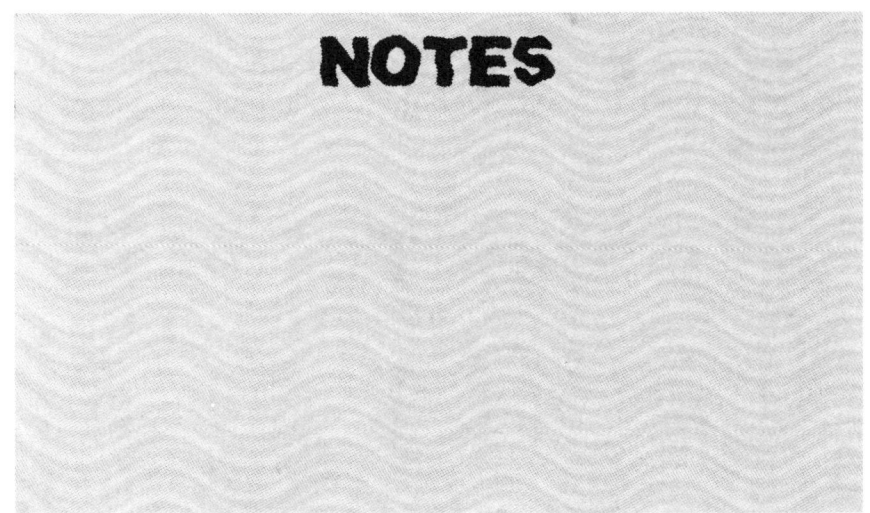

Bible Bonus Note:

The Hebrew noun *Elohim* in Genesis 1:1 is used over 2,200 times in the Old Testament as one of the names of God. Interestingly, it is a plural noun that uses a singular verb, which some interpreters believe hints at the plurality within the unity of God. One of the New Testament verses that expresses this truth is Matthew 28:19: "Therefore, go and make disciples of all nations, baptizing them in the name [singular] of the Father and of the Son and of the Holy Spirit [plural]."

This New Testament understanding of God as the Trinity contrasts with the Jewish interpretation of the name of God based upon Deuteronomy 6:4: "Hear, O Israel: The LORD our God, the LORD is one." But even in this verse, the word for "one" (*eschad*) can be used in a plural way, just as the plurality of grapes within the unity of one cluster in

Bible Bonus Note: (Cont'd.)

Numbers 13:23.
It is striking that in the first verse of the Bible, God already gives hints that He cannot be reduced to something we can easily understand, namely a single divinity. Rather, throughout Scripture God reveals Himself as a threefold God whose unity can never be totally comprehended by our limited human minds. But aren't you glad we serve a God who is bigger than we can understand? If we could understand Him, He'd be reduced to just a pretty cool guy, but He wouldn't be our blessed Creator and Redeemer.

Review and Approach

15 MINUTES

OBJECTIVE
To help students remember the key concepts in the creation story.

MATERIALS AND PREPARATION NEEDED
Zip, nada—nothin' but your good looks!

Greet students and divide them into two teams. Try using creative team divisions, such as their choice between two favorite fast-food restaurants, two favorite television shows, or two of their favorite qualities of your teaching (although this might be difficult because there are bound to be *so* many!).

Explain that you're going to start today with a singing game. The game is simple: You will say the following words or phrases one at a time and the teams will take turns singing a lyric from a song that includes the word or phrase. Students can use either Christian or secular songs, but each song can only be used once during the game. The team that outlasts the other will get 1,000 points. Use the following seven words or phrases:

God	love
you	earth or ground
water or sea	good
any kind of animal	

When the game is finished, ask: **What do all of these words have in common?** They're all part of the last session's Creation story from Genesis 1. **Who can put them into one sentence that summarizes everything we learned last time?**

Today we're going to take an even closer look at how God made the earth and everything in it, including people! Including us!

Bible Exploration Two

30 MINUTES

OBJECTIVE
To allow students to see the perfection of God's creation plan.

MATERIALS AND PREPARATION NEEDED
- ❑ A Bible
- ❑ White board and marker or chalkboard and chalk
- ❑ A table
- ❑ A lamp
- ❑ Anything blue
- ❑ A bag of dirt
- ❑ A plant (real or fake)
- ❑ A pitcher of water
- ❑ A pair of sunglasses and/or suntan lotion
- ❑ A large stuffed animal

Ahead of time, set up the table at the front of the room.

Have students remain in the two teams from the Review and Approach activity and explain that you're going to read the Scripture passage for today, Genesis 1:1—2:3. Instruct them to listen carefully, because afterward you're going to ask them some trivia questions based on what it says. Read the passage and then ask the following questions, *making sure to keep score on the board of which team answers each correctly*:

1. **Light—On what day did God create light?** The first day.
2. **Sky—True or False: The Bible specifically mentions the word "sky."** True (at least the *NIV* does).
3. **Land and plants—What did all the plants and trees have?** Seeds.
4. **Sun and moon—Which light governed the night, the greater light or the lesser light?** The lesser.
5. **Fish and birds—True or False: The passage we read mentions specific kinds of fish, but not specific kinds of birds.** False.
6. **Animals and man—Does the Bible passage that we read mention Eve?** No.

Congratulate the teams for their answers; then ask for a representative from each team to come forward for the team's prizes. Give the representatives the prizes that correspond to each day that their team guessed correctly and tell them to hold onto each prize.

Prizes:
1. Light—lamp
2. Sky—the blue "thing"
3. Land and plants—bag of dirt and plant
4. Sun and moon—suntan lotion and sunglasses
5. Fish and birds—stuffed animal
6. Animals and man—ask another student to come and jump into the arms of the team representative—this "prize" represents Adam.

> **Note:** To prevent possible injuries, the student who will be receiving the Animals and Man "prize" needs to be physically capable of catching him or her, so keep this in mind when selecting both the team representative and the "prize"!

The goal of giving these prizes is to overwhelm both team representatives with all their "prizes." By now, at least one, if not both, of the students should be overwhelmed. Comment on this and explain: **Even though we could never handle all that was created in Genesis 1, our God can.**

Ask the two representatives to put all their prizes on the table in the front of the room; then ask students on both teams to work together to put the props in chronological order of how God created them (yes, including the actual junior higher who is representing Adam). Explain as you point to each prop: God's creation plan is absolutely perfect. If these had been created in any different order, it wouldn't have worked. Fish needed a sea to swim in; Adam needed air to breathe; the birds, animals and humans needed plants for food. God was completely in control of His creation and not a single error was made. He created everything in perfect order, and all of the parts came together just as they were supposed to.

Ask: Think about our bodies. How do human hands show the perfection of God's plan? The fact that they have five fingers that can bend and work together are perfect for all of the jobs we need our hands to do.

What about our eyes—how do they show the perfection of God's plan? The optic nerve and shape of our eyes allow us to see the vivid shapes and colors and images around us.

What else in creation shows God's perfect plan? As students give answers, take each answer and explain that if even one small part of that part of creation was changed, it wouldn't work as well.

Conclusion and Decision

 15 MINUTES

OBJECTIVE
To help students feel secure knowing that God made them especially unique and loves them as they are.

MATERIALS AND PREPARATION NEEDED
- ❑ Pens or pencils
- ❑ Copies of "Dear Me" (p. 22)
- ❑ **Option:** Copies of this session's memory verse, Genesis 1:1,27 on the "Memory Mania" handout (p. 23)

> **OPTION—Memory Mania:** Distribute copies of the memory verse (if you haven't already done so) and challenge students to memorize the verse before the next meeting. The reproducible student handout "Memory Mania" (p. 23) contains the memory verses for using this course as a five-session study. You can give the whole page of verses to the students now or you can cut the verses apart and give one at each session
> **Note:** If you plan to use all 10 sessions in this study, additional memory verses are provided in "Memory Mania II" (p. 24). These alternate verses could also be used for an additional challenge for a five-session study.
> **Suggestion:** Give daily prizes to students who memorize their verses each day and perhaps a special treat or prize to those who memorize all of the verses.

Ask volunteers to read the following verses:
"God saw all that He had made, and it was very good" (Genesis 1:31).
"I praise you because I am fearfully and wonderfully made; your works are wonderful, I know that full well" (Psalm 139:14).
"The Lord will fulfill his purpose for me" (Psalm 138:8).
Discuss:
What do these verses tell us about God's view of us? He has made us special and good, and there is a reason for our being here on earth.
If it is true that God's creation is good and He created us, what does that say about us? Accept a variety of answers.
What is further evidence of how special you are to God? He sent His Son to die for us; He takes care of us; etc.
Distribute pens or pencils and a copy of "Dear Me" to each student and ask them to choose words from the border of the handout to fill in the blanks to describe how God feels about

them. Encourage students to keep their "Dear Me" letters on their bathroom or bedroom mirrors or in their Bibles as constant reminders of how God feels about them.

Hand out the memory verses and explain: **In each session you're going to be getting a memory verse. Each memory verse is important for us to learn because it provides a great one-sentence summary of each session. The memory verse for this session is Genesis 1:1,27: "In the beginning God created the heavens and the earth. So God created man in his own image, in the image of God he created him; male and female he created them."** Spend a minute or two helping students understand the meaning of the verse; then challenge them to memorize the verse. (**Note:** If you are dividing this session into two sessions give students the alternate verse after the second session.)

Close in prayer, thanking God for the comfort of knowing that since we are His creation, we know that He has made us a perfect 10. Ask students to thank God for one special quality, ability or blessing He has given them in simple one-sentence prayers.

Word Up

EMPTY GROUND PLANT IMAGE	ANIMALS STARS SEA LIGHT
WATER SKY INCREASE FRUIT	WILD DRY DARK MORNING
FISH NUMBER MOVES BREATH	LIFE HEAVENS REST BIRDS

Dear Me

If this were a letter from God, pick words from the border of this sheet to describe what He would say about you, His good and perfect creation.

AWESOME BEAUTIFUL HANDSOME TALENTED HELPFUL FRIENDLY GIFTED PRETTY GOOD FUN SMART KIND CUTE UNIQUE LOVABLE PERFECT VALUABLE SPECIAL WONDERFUL DEPENDABLE

Dear _____,

I just want you to know that I love you. I think you're _____. From the moment you were born, I've thought that you are very _____. There's nothing I'd change about you. You're much more _____ and _____ than you even realize.

You are My wonderful creation and thinking about you makes Me smile.

Love,
God

© 1999 by Gospel Light. Permission to photocopy granted. *GP4U (God's Plan for You)*

Memory Mania

EPHESIANS 5:2 — And live a life of love, just as Christ loved us and gave himself up for us as a fragrant offering and sacrifice to God.

---

1 PETER 3:18 — For Christ died for sins once for all, the righteous for the unrighteous, to bring you to God. He was put to death in the body but made alive by the Spirit.

JOHN 14:6,7 — Jesus answered, I am the way and the truth and the life. No one comes to the Father except through me. If you really knew me, you would know my Father as well. From now on, you do know him and have seen him.

ROMANS 3:23 — For all have sinned and fall short of the glory of God.

GENESIS 1:1,27 — In the beginning God created the heavens and the earth. So God created man in his own image, in the image of God he created him; male and female he created them.

© 1999 by Gospel Light. Permission to photocopy granted. *GP4U (God's Plan for You)*

Memory Mania II

ACTS 1:8

But you will receive power when the Holy Spirit comes on you; and you will be my witnesses in Jerusalem, and in all Judea and Samaria, and to the ends of the earth.

LUKE 24:5-7

Why do you look for the living among the dead? He is not here; he has risen! Remember how he told you, while he was still with you in Galilee: The Son of Man must be delivered into the hands of sinful men, be crucified and on the third day be raised again.

JOHN 1:1,2,14

In the beginning was the Word, and the Word was with God, and the Word was God. He was with God in the beginning. The Word became flesh and made his dwelling among us. We have seen his glory, the glory of the One and Only, who came from the Father, full of grace and truth.

ROMANS 3:10-12

There is no one righteous, not even one; there is no one who understands, no one who seeks God. All have turned away, they have together become worthless; there is no one who does good, not even one.

PSALM 139:14

I praise you because I am fearfully and wonderfully made; your works are wonderful, I know that full well.

© 1999 by Gospel Light. Permission to photocopy granted. *GP4U (God's Plan for You)*

SESSION 2

Our Only Roadblock

Leader's Devotional

Katie Magridichian was tired of her mom nagging at her. First, her mom wanted her to clean her room because her grandparents were coming over (not that they ever saw her room in the first place, as Katie pointed out to her mom). Next, she had fallen behind in her seventh grade math homework and her mom was making her study before she even picked up the phone or E-mailed any of her friends.

Then Katie's mom had reached the final straw. She noticed that Katie had a sniffle and jumped to the conclusion that Katie had some kind of dangerous and potentially life-threatening illness. She had made a doctor's appointment for the following day—a *Saturday*, so Katie didn't even get to miss any school for it! "Mom, it's no big deal. It's just a sniffle," Katie argued. But her mom wouldn't change her mind.

The doctor examined Katie and said she had a minor infection. He gave her a prescription for some antibiotics. Her mom brought home the medicine from the neighborhood drugstore, but Katie took it only a few times. She kept forgetting to take it before school, and by the time she remembered at night, she was already in bed and didn't feel like walking downstairs to the kitchen.

Now imagine what would've happened if Katie knew she was really sick, and she had been the one to beg her mom to take her to the doctor's office. The doctor would still give her a prescription, but how would Katie respond? She would rush with her mom to the drugstore to get the medicine and never miss a single pill.

What's the difference? In the first situation, Katie doesn't really think she's sick, in the second she does. In the first situation, Katie is apathetic; in the second she is insistent.

The goal of this session is to show students that they have a sickness—not a physical sickness, but a spiritual one. They are born in sin and remain separated from God. This is no minor cold, but an illness that sentences them to a hellish life in their present life and a literal hell after their death. Hopefully, this session will leave students wanting the solution—a solution that is found in Jesus Christ alone.

Session 2 Our Only Roadblock

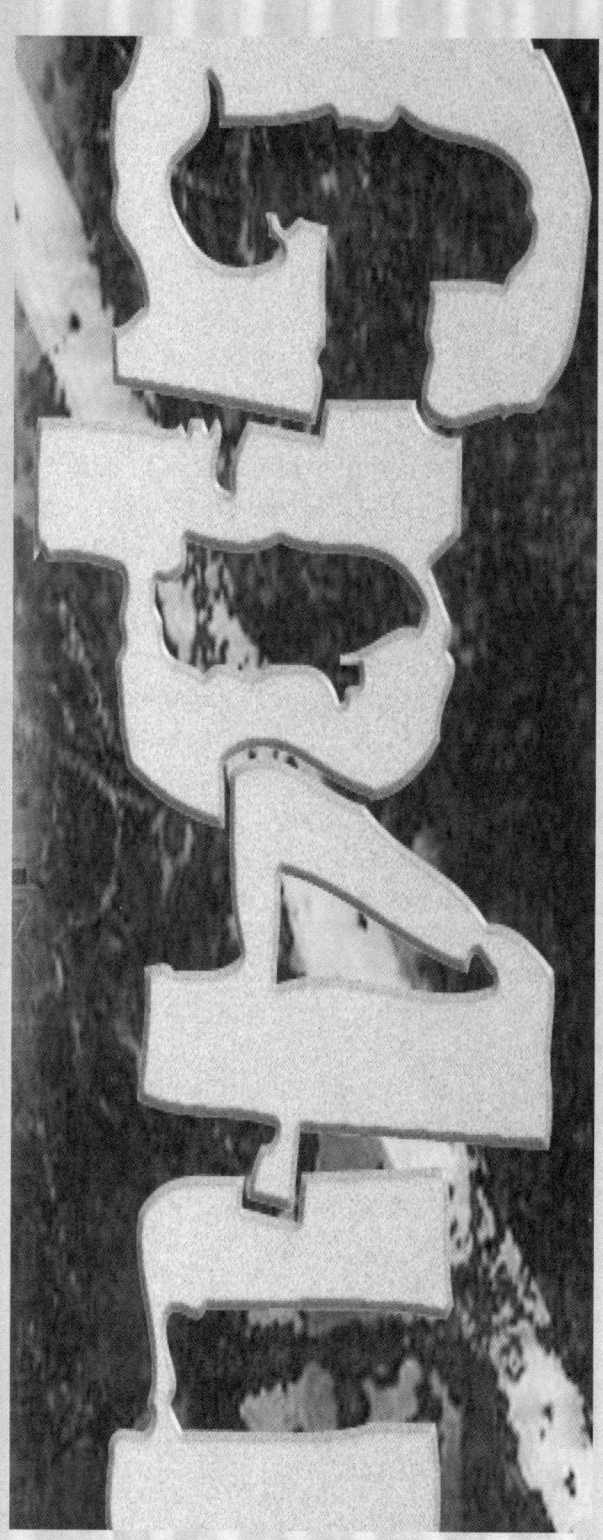

Key Verse

"When the woman saw that the fruit of the tree was good for food and pleasing to the eye, and also desirable for gaining wisdom, she took some and ate it. She also gave some to her husband, who was with her, and he ate it. Then the eyes of both of them were opened, and they realized they were naked; so they sewed fig leaves together and made coverings for themselves." Genesis 3:6,7

Biblical Basis

Genesis 2:8,9,15,16; 3:1-24; John 9:1-3; Romans 3:10-12,23

Focus of This Session

Sin separates us from God.

Aims of This Session

During this session students will:
- Learn about the benefits of having choices about what to do, even though that means we can choose to sin;
- Feel the power of their sinful desire to do the wrong thing;
- Act by identifying specific sins they struggle with.

Approach the Word

20 MINUTES

OBJECTIVE
To teach students to be glad that God gives them choices, even though that means they can choose to sin.

MATERIALS AND PREPARATION NEEDED
- ❑ Enough chairs for every student
- ❑ One water bottle or glass of water for each student
- ❑ One can or glass of soda for each student

Greet students and let them know how glad you are that they showed up today. Explain that you're going to begin today by playing the "Been-There-Done-That Circle Game."[1] Ask students to set up a circle of chairs. Count the number of students and make sure you have one less chair than the number of participants.

In the center of the circle, one student stands and shares something about herself, such as "I've been to the Grand Canyon." Anyone who has *not* been to the Grand Canyon must get up and run for another chair. The person in the middle then has the opportunity to sit down in the circle. One important rule: Students may not move to chairs on either side of them when they are vacated. They must get up and run across for another chair. When the chairs are full, the student remaining standing becomes It and must tell something about himself that other students have probably not done.

When you have finished the game, congratulate all of the students and say that you have drinks for everyone. Ask the students in one half of the room to come forward first as you give them all a bottle or glass of water. Next, ask the second half of the room to come as you give them the chance to choose either water or soda. This will undoubtedly provoke a chorus of, "Hey, wait a minute. We only got water!" from the first group of students. This is *exactly* what you want to happen!

Once students settle down, allow students who were in the first half the chance to get a soda if they'd like. Explain: **We tend to like choices because they give us options of what to do. From choices of drinks to choices of clothes to choices of television shows, we like to be able to pick, instead of feeling like we don't have a choice.**

Reminder:
Don't forget Memory Mania!

In the last session we studied our Creator God. Not only did He create us and give us the world, He gives us the freedom to choose many things. He allows us to be more than robots. The one problem we have with choices is that they give us the chance to pick the *wrong* thing. When we choose to do the wrong thing, it's called a sin. But sin isn't just *doing* wrong things; it involves an attitude of wanting to live our lives without God, doing things our own way or openly rebelling against Him. Today we're going to look at the reason that we often choose to do the wrong thing and how we can make the choice to do the right thing.

Bible Exploration One

30 MINUTES

OBJECTIVE
To help students experience the power of their own sin.

MATERIALS AND PREPARATION NEEDED
- ❏ Your Bible
- ❏ Candy prizes
- ❏ A table
- ❏ Bowls filled with the following food: carrot slices, celery slices, apple slices and pieces of bittersweet chocolate
- ❏ Napkins or paper towels.

> **Note:** You can purchase bittersweet chocolate at your local grocery store in the baking aisle and break it into pieces as you would a candy bar.

Ahead of time, cue the members of your adult team that if students want to disobey your instructions not to eat the chocolate and sneak a bite, the adults should pretend not to notice.

Place the bowls of food on the table, and then explain: **I've brought some snacks for us to share, but I have to step out to make a phone call** (or make a copy, do a brain transplant—whatever). **You can have the carrots, apples and celery slices, but don't eat any of the chocolate. It's for later.** Be sure to *not* tell students that it's actually bittersweet chocolate.

Leave the room for a couple of minutes. Come back in the room and ask students: **How did you like the snacks? Did any of you try the chocolate?** If the answer is yes (which is the most likely answer), ask students how it tasted. If the answer is no, congratulate students on their obedience and give them a sample of the bittersweet chocolate. Either way, they'll think the chocolate is pretty disgusting. Explain: **When we disobey rules, although the sins might look appealing, we often regret the taste it leaves in our mouths—literally!**

Explain that you're going to read a story in the Bible that relates to this activity. Instruct students to listen for any similarities between the Genesis story of sin and the food temptation while you read. If they hear any, they should stand up, interrupt you to share it, and then you'll give that student a piece of candy. Likely similarities include: resemblances between you and God (yes, that was a joke), there is one thing they were told not to eat, the temptation looked attractive, we tend to want to hide any sin we've committed, and the consequences of sin are painful.

After you've read Genesis 2:8,9,15,16 and 3:1-24, explain: **The most common New Testament word for "sin" was a word from archery and literally means "missing the mark." If you took the chocolate, you missed the mark, and look how bad it tasted. How does sin leave a bad taste in our mouths?** Allow students to respond with some of the negative consequences of sin.

Continue: **Isn't it interesting that the serpent asked Eve, "Did God really say...?" in Genesis 3:1? It's often our doubt in who God is and His promises to us that cause us to stray from what He wants us to do. If we *really* knew the goodness of God that we talked about in the last session and didn't doubt His plans for us, we'd be much more able to stop sinning.**

> **Note:** If you are completing this session in one meeting, skip to "Conclusion and Decision."

Warning:

You may want to have napkins or paper towels available for students to spit out the chocolate.

30 Session 2

Two-Meeting Track: If you want to spread this session over two meetings, STOP here and close in prayer. Inform students of the content to be covered in your next meeting.

Review and Approach

Objective
To show students that every person who has lived has sinned—except one: Jesus Christ.

Materials and Preparation Needed
- ❏ Scissors
- ❏ Copies of "I Never!" (p. 34)
- ❏ **Option:** Copies of this session's memory verse, Romans 3:23 on the "Memory Mania" handout (p. 23)

Ahead of time, cut apart the "I Never!" handouts so that every student has at least three "I Never!" squares.

Welcome students and explain that you're going to start with a game that helps students discover some pretty weird truths about each other. Divide students into groups of 10 and give each student three "I Never!" squares. Explain: **One at a time, go around the circle and think of something you've never done, such as "I've never been able to whistle" or "I've never been water skiing" or "I've never washed my youth leader's car." The goal is to come up with something that you've NEVER done that lots of others in your circle have done, which may make the "I've never washed my youth leader's car" a poor sentence. Anyway, once a person makes an "I Never!" statement, anyone who *has* done that thing has to put an "I Never!" square in the center of the circle. The goal is to be the last one left with "I Never!" squares.**

Reminder:

Don't forget Memory Mania!

Let this continue for about 10 minutes; then congratulate anyone who still has "I Never!" squares left. Ask: **Can anyone think of an "I Never!" statement that no human alive could ever make?** If students need a hint, explain: **Jesus could make this "I Never!" statement, but no one else could.** The answer is that no one could ever say "I never sinned." Explain: **Every single person, regardless of their background or how much money they have or where they live, has one thing in common: we've all sinned, against God and against other people. All of us. Every single one. Our memory verse for today makes this pretty clear. In Romans 3:23, Paul wrote, "All have sinned and fall short of the glory of God." Today we're going to continue to figure out how we all came to be full of sin.**

Bible Exploration Two

30 MINUTES

OBJECTIVE
To show students that sin separates us from God.

MATERIALS AND PREPARATION NEEDED
- A Bible
- Ice cubes
- Water
- Vegetable oil
- A clear glass bowl
- A pen or pencil
- A piece of paper
- A grocery bag
- A two- to four-minute video clip from the local news
- A TV and a VCR
- One copy of "Sin Situations" (p. 35), cut into three sections

Note: Be sure to practice the object lesson ahead of time.

Ahead of time, videotape a two- to four-minute segment from the local news showing people who have been caught doing something wrong.

Summarize Genesis 2:8,9,15,16 in your own words. Ask volunteers to read the verses in Genesis 3:1-24 aloud. Use the following object lesson to illustrate how the sin of disobeying God separated Adam and Eve from God:

Pour the water and ice cubes into the clear glass bowl and explain: **The water represents Adam and Eve and the ice represents God. Even though the water and ice are separate things, yet with the ice floating on the water, they can still touch each other.** Now pour in vegetable oil. The oil will float to the top between the water and the ice cubes. Continue: **The oil is like sin, and sin separates Adam and Eve (the water) from God (the ice cubes). The sin from Adam and Eve didn't stop where it began in the Garden of Eden. It's been passed down by every generation from them to us, thousands of years later. We, too, are like the water and are separated by our sin, or the oil, from God. Since sin was passed from Adam to us, we all now walk around with sin inside of us, wanting to do our own thing. It contaminates everything we do and every thought we have. I've got a news clip and I want you to watch for examples of sin.**

Play the two- to four-minute news clip and ask students to share how they saw sin's result in the news stories, such as someone who committed a murder or someone who started a fire. Read John 9:1-3 to make sure students understand that every bad thing that happens is *not* a result of that person's sin, or his or her parents' or stepparents' sin for that matter. Explain to them that we live in a broken world, still reeling from the effects of Adam's wrong choice (see Romans 5:12). However, all sins are the result of *the* sin that causes our hearts to be naturally bent toward evil. We don't have to be taught how to do wrong things. It comes naturally to us because of the condition of our sinful hearts.

Bring the point closer to home by selecting three pairs of students to act out different scenarios. Explain that you are going to give each pair a scenario and one person in each pair will be the actor and the other will be the voice double. The voice double will read the monologue while the actor mouths the words and simultaneously acts them out.

Give each pair their scenario and relevant prop (Situation 1: The Bible; Situation 2: The pen and paper; Situation 3: The grocery bag). Following each situation, ask: **How is sin involved in what the person did?** After everyone has completed their scenario, ask: **Can you think of anything we do that isn't motivated by some kind of gain, whether it be money, attention, looking good, or even feeling good about ourselves? Our sin is so deep inside us that it colors everything we think and do.**

Conclusion and Decision

 15 MINUTES

OBJECTIVE
To help students identify sins they struggle with.

MATERIALS AND PREPARATIONS NEEDED
- Pens or pencils
- Copies of "Heart Attack" (p. 36)
- An overhead projector and marker
- An overhead transparency copy of "Heart Attack" (p. 36)

Place the "Heart Attack" overhead transparency on the projector and explain: **This represents our heart which, although it was created by God, has now been filled with our sin. Here are some of my sins.** At this point, write some of your sins directly on the overhead transparency (such as pride, greed, jealousy, lust or anger, etc.). Share vulnerably, but remember that you're the adult in the room. Distribute pens or pencils and copies of "Heart Attack" as you explain: **Sin has attacked our hearts, and on this handout, I want you to write down some of your own sins.** Give students a few minutes to write down their sins. Read Romans 3:23 and remind them: **None of us are alone in our sins. Everyone else in this room has sinned, too—and sins every day.**

Close in prayer, asking God to help us all overcome our sins so that we can make right choices.

Note
1. Adapted from Jim Burns, *Fresh Ideas 3: Games, Crowdbreakers and Community Builders* (Ventura, CA: Gospel Light, 1997), p. 24.

I Never!

I NEVER!	I NEVER!	I NEVER!	I NEVER!
I never!	I never!	I never!	I never!
I never!	I never!	I never!	I never!
I never!	I never!	I never!	I never!
I never!	I never!	I never!	I never!

© 1999 by Gospel Light. Permission to photocopy granted. *GP4U (God's Plan for You)*

Sin Situations

Situation 1

My small group at church is pretty cool. We talk about what's going on at school and stuff. I think my favorite thing about my small group is the leader. She is so cool. She has us over to spend the night at her college dorm room and introduces us to all her friends. The only thing I'd change about her is that I wish she wouldn't ask us every time if we've read our Bible passage during the past week. I know some other people in the group lie so that they don't disappoint her. I never lie, but unfortunately I never read my Bible, so I'm always letting her down. This week is different, though. I read through the passage three times. I can't wait to tell her.

Situation 2

I am so tired of my little brother. All he does is nag, nag, nag. "Come and play with me" or "Come and talk to me." Nag, nag, nag. I just wish he'd find some friends his own age instead of trying to hang out with me and my friends. Why doesn't he find friends his own size? And why doesn't he stay out of my room? One time I even caught him looking through my CDs, although he denied that was what he was doing. The only way I know to keep him quiet is to help him with his math homework. Every once in a while I let him draw on my arm, just for fun. That seems to keep him busy, plus he feels like I'm paying attention to him. At least a little bit.

Situation 3

My mom has really been on my case lately. "Clean the floor" or "Empty the dishwasher" seem like the only things she ever says to me. Last week before she even said "Hello," she told me I needed to clean up the living room before grandma and grandpa came over. At least yesterday I scored some points. When she drove home in the minivan, I could see grocery bags inside the windows. Instead of running over to our neighbor's house like I usually do so that I wouldn't have to unload the groceries, I decided that I could get her off my back if I volunteered to help. So I did. And I saw some cookies in the bag and I didn't even take any.

© 1999 by Gospel Light. Permission to photocopy granted. *GP4U (God's Plan for You)*

Heart Attack

In this heart, write the sins that you struggle with in your own life.

© 1999 by Gospel Light. Permission to photocopy granted. *GP4U (God's Plan for You)*

SESSION 3

One Way Only

Leader's Devotional

One Friday morning, you receive a phone call from a family that has recently moved to your town. They've called you because they want to bring their daughter to your youth ministry on Sunday and they need directions to your church. There are two ways to get from their house to your church, either by the main highway or by the city streets. You ask them which they would prefer, and since they say they would prefer to drive on the highway, you give them the first set of directions.

If this same family checked a map of their own, they might discover another way to get to your church. And if their daughter checked an internet navigational system, she might discover yet a fourth way to get there. Yet it really doesn't matter, does it, as long as all four roads lead to the same place?

Well, if you're talking about a simple drive to church, then you're right. But if you're talking about the way to salvation, then you're *wrong*.

Our cultural emphasis on relativism and tolerance has crept its way into our churches and into our students' minds. For many people, Jesus is simply one of several ways to get to God. Others might say, "He may be the best way for *you*, but that doesn't mean He's the best way for *me*."

This session shatters that lie. The essence of all Scripture can be distilled to one well-known, often-memorized statement by Jesus, "For God so loved the world that He gave His one and only son, that whoever believes in Him shall not perish but have eternal life" (John 3:16). A few chapters later, Jesus states His one-of-a-kind-ness even more clearly in the memory verse for this session, "I am the way and the truth and the life. No one comes to the Father except through me" (John 14:6). Jesus is not merely *a* way to get to the Father; He is *the* way—the *only* way! There aren't several roads you can choose from based on your own preferences and moods; there is only one—His name is Jesus. This session gives us the chance to clear away the confusing rhetoric about the "many ways" to get to God and clearly point students to the One Way Only road named Jesus Christ.

Session 3 One Way Only

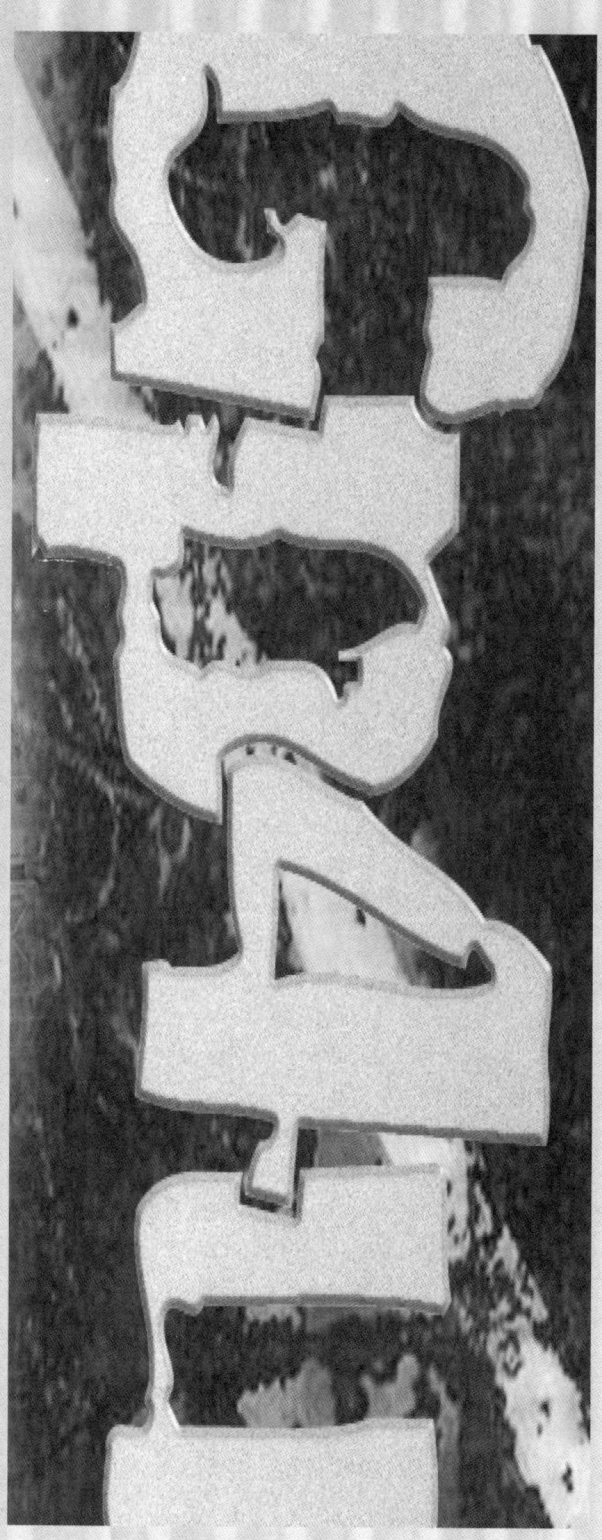

Key Verse

"Jesus answered, 'I am the way and the truth and the life. No one comes to the Father except through me. If you really knew me, you would know my Father as well.'" John 14:6,7

Biblical Basis

John 1:1,2,14; 5:1-9; 6:16-21; 14:1-7

Focus of This Session

God's son, Jesus, gives us a clear picture of what God is like.

Aims of This Session

During this session students will:
- Understand that there is only one way to God—Jesus Christ;
- Feel closer to God by understanding the actions of His Son;
- Act by recognizing at least one thing that Jesus is capable of doing in their lives.

Approach the Word

15 MINUTES

OBJECTIVE
To help students understand that it's easier to describe people with a picture.

MATERIALS AND PREPARATION NEEDED
- Pens or pencils
- Paper
- Copies of "All About Me" (p. 46)
- A large bowl or bucket

Greet students and ask them how they are doing. Explain that you're going to start this session with a game to see how well people know each other. Distribute copies of "All About Me" and pens or pencils. Instruct students that when they've finished completing the handouts, they should fold them up and put them in the bowl or bucket that you've placed at the front of the room.

Explain as you distribute blank sheets of paper: **Now we're going to see how much we know about each other. I'm going to choose one of these papers and read a few of the person's answers without reading the person's actual name. I'll try to choose answers that are somewhat vague and won't make the person's identity too obvious. Write down who you think it is on the paper I'm giving you. We'll do this several times, and then I'll read all the correct identities. If I choose your paper, try to look innocent and don't let anyone else know it's you.**

After you've read the answers, discuss: **Was this game hard or easy? What would have been some questions I could have included that would make it easier? What about if I had shown you a picture of the person? You probably could have guessed who it was for sure.**

Continue: **We've already studied how God created all of us and made us good and unique. We've also studied how each of us has sinned by turning away from God. Today we're going to look a little closer at who God is by looking at His son, Jesus Christ. Jesus Christ is like a snapshot of God that shows us exactly what God is like. If we study what Jesus did and what He said, we'll never have to guess about what God is like.**

Reminder:

Don't forget Memory Mania!

Bible Exploration One

30 MINUTES

OBJECTIVE
To show students that Jesus is the way to God and the way to know what God is like.

MATERIALS AND PREPARATION NEEDED
- ❏ Several Bibles
- ❏ A complete set of fast-food items (such as french fries from one fast-food joint, pizza from another, hamburgers from another) for every 5 to 10 students
- ❏ Adult volunteers to head each team of 5 to 10 students
- ❏ Copies of your scavenger hunt clues
- ❏ **Option:** Copies of this session's memory verse, John 14:6,7 on the "Memory Mania" handout (p. 23)

Ahead of time, decide where you are going to hide the food; then write down one clue about each location. For example: "Being around little kids can fry your brain," (i.e., french fries in the nursery), or "Sometimes people walking into church sound like they're afraid," (i.e., chicken in the lobby). **Note:** Hide only one type of the food in each room and make sure to hide it out of sight. Photocopy enough copies of the clues for every 5 to 10 students you expect at your meeting. On each copy, randomly number the clues, from 1 to 3, designating the order that each team must follow to find the food. This will keep them from merely following each other around. In this kind of fast-food scavenger hunt, it's fun to bump into each other, but it's a pain to be trapped in one big caravan.

> **Note:** If your church would frown on fast food in the sanctuary, make sure to avoid it, along with any other controversial places (such as your senior pastor's office).

Ask: **Is anyone here hungry? Does anyone want to do a fast-food scavenger hunt? Which of you has a driver's license and a car with them? Oh, that's right; you're junior highers—you don't drive yet. I guess we'll just have to do it here!**

Divide students into the same number of teams that you purchased fast-food sets for and that you have instructions for. Explain that each team must start at the clue marked 1 and follow the rest of the clues in order. When they find the fast food, they can take one *and only one* item with them as they head to the next clue. And yes, they can eat along the way. Try to assign an adult to each team to help corral students and keep them from destroying any church property, such as that revered organ in your worship center.

After all of the teams have returned, explain: **Without the clues, some of you would still be running around. We all need clues about where to go. Today we're going to study Jesus Christ, who gives us a picture of what God is like as well as how to get to God. Without Him, we'd be lost and running around confused. Knowing Him shows us the right steps to take.**

Have a volunteer read John 1:1,2,14; then discuss:

Who is the Word? Jesus.

Is Jesus older or younger than God? Jesus is the same age as God; they've both been around since before the beginning of time.

What happened to the Word? He became flesh and moved into our neighborhood here on earth.

Next, have a volunteer read John 14:1-7; then discuss the following questions:

What does Jesus mean by "my Father's house"? Heaven.

What "I am" statements does Jesus make and what do they mean? I am going there to prepare a place for you, meaning Jesus is preparing a way for us to get to heaven. And, I am the way and the truth and the life, meaning Jesus is the only way to God.

According to John 14:1-7, are there many ways to get to God? No, Jesus is the *only* way.

If Thomas came to you and still didn't understand what Jesus meant, what would you tell him?

How is this different from what other religions teach about getting to God, heaven or salvation? Other religions say that salvation is based on what you do, meaning your works and good deeds, or who you are, meaning how good you are. The Bible teaches us that what we are and what we do is filled with sin. The way to heaven is based on who we know: Jesus Christ as the *only* way to heaven. Read John 14:6,7 aloud. Encourage students to memorize John 14:6,7 before the next session as a great explanation of the belief that no one can come to God the Father except through Jesus. Ask: **Do you want to know the Father? You need to come to Him through Jesus.**

Note: If you are completing this session in one meeting, skip to "Conclusion and Decision."

Two-Meeting Track: If you want to spread this session over two meetings, STOP here and close in prayer. Inform students of the content to be covered in your next meeting.

Review and Approach

15 MINUTES

OBJECTIVE
To show students that Jesus can do anything.

MATERIALS AND PREPARATION NEEDED
- Pens or pencils
- Copies of "Can It" (p. 47)
- Candy prizes

Reminder: Don't forget Memory Mania!

Distribute copies of "Can It" and pens or pencils. Announce that you have prizes for everyone that gets six in a row (up, down or diagonal). If you have fewer than 15 people, allow students to sign their initials in two boxes, instead of just one. Encourage students to actually demonstrate what they can do if it's at all possible in the meeting place.

After everyone has finished, ask: **Do you know anyone who can do all of these things? Probably not. Can you think of anyone who can do all of these things? The only person I can think of is God.**

Continue: **We've already learned that Jesus gives us a picture of what God is like and gives us the way to get to Him. Today we're going to look at a few more pictures of Jesus and see what they tell us about God. I think you'll be pretty impressed at some of the remarkable things Jesus can do.**

Bible Exploration Two

30 MINUTES

OBJECTIVE
To help students see Jesus' sovereignty and power.

MATERIALS AND PREPARATION NEEDED
- ❏ Several Bibles
- ❏ Pens or pencils
- ❏ Paper
- ❏ One large piece of poster board
- ❏ A large felt-tip pen
- ❏ Two white boards (or two easels with lots of newsprint paper)
- ❏ Copies of "Twin Stories" (p. 48)

Ahead of time, place the white boards (or easels) on opposite sides of the room.

Divide students into two teams (we'll call them "boys" and "girls" to make the explanation simpler, but you might want to come up with other creative team divisions) and assign each team a white board. Ask for one volunteer from each team to come to the front as you whisper the word "lake" into their ears. They must then run back to the white board and draw a lake (or whatever resembles a lake) until their team guesses the correct word. Continue this with different volunteer pairs using the following additional words: "boat," "wind," "row," "shore," "pool," "columns" and "mat." Keep a running total of points on a piece of poster board giving 1,000 points to the team who guesses each correct answer first.

Console the team that is behind by letting them know they have two more chances to catch up. You're going to read two stories from Scripture, and whenever they hear you read any of the eight words that were drawn, they should stand up. If they're the first one to stand up and they're right, their team gets 500 points; if they're wrong, they lose 1,000 points. Read John 5:1-9 and 6:16-21 aloud, and you're sure to have a roomful of eager ears. **Hint:** Have another adult help you keep track of the scores.

Let the team that is behind know that they still have a chance to catch up. Distribute Bibles and copies of "Twin Stories" and instruct students to write down any similarities between the two stories listed on the handout. Allow several minutes to do this; then ask the groups to share their answers. Award 500 points for every valid similarity that the teams discovered. Congratulate the winning team, and then comment: **Since Jesus was God when He walked this earth, He had the same control and power that God did. Whether it be a huge storm or a crippled man, Jesus could change the situation. He changed lives wherever He went, and the same is still true. He changes the life of anyone who meets or sees Him.**

Important note: Be sensitive to your students' spiritual needs. This might be the time to give students an opportunity to respond to the salvation offered by Jesus Christ. This step is actually suggested in Session 4, but if you feel it is appropriate here, go for it! There is a reproducible resource—"How to Get to Know Jesus"—at the end of this book (pp. 77-78) to help you lead young people to the Lord.

If you feel the Holy Spirit is guiding you to do so, at this point in the session tell students that if anyone would like to learn more about how to come to know Jesus Christ as Savior and make Him Lord of their lives, to speak to you after the session. Or with heads bowed, ask students to raise their hands to let you know they would like to talk to you. You could also make an overhead transparency of "How to Get to Know Jesus" and take the whole group through the steps.

Conclusion and Decision

15 MINUTES

OBJECTIVE
To help students understand the remarkable things that Jesus can do in their lives.

MATERIALS AND PREPARATION NEEDED
- Pens or pencils
- Copies of "Jesus, You Can…" (p. 49)

Ahead of time, ask a few students to share brief two- to three-minute testimonies of some remarkable things they've seen Jesus do in their lives. It can range from finding their dad a job to helping their stepmom with her back problems to helping them have boldness to share knowledge about the Bible in their English class. **Hint:** Select students that you know have had definite answers to prayer.

> **Note:** With junior highers, it's *imperative* to review their testimonies in advance to make sure they tell *specific* stories (talking about more than just "stuff" and "things") and are *on track* (avoiding some of those notorious junior high tangents).

Explain: **Jesus didn't just change the lives of people back in Bible times. He continues to change our lives today. I've asked a few of our friends to share ways that they've seen Jesus do some amazing things in their own lives.**

After the prepared students share and *if the mood seems right*, ask if any other students have stories about what Jesus has done that they'd like to share. Otherwise move right ahead to the closing activity by distributing a pen or pencil and a copy of "Jesus, You Can…" to each student. Explain that Jesus, as God, can do anything. He is all powerful. Give students a few minutes to write down something that they know Jesus can do in their lives given what they've learned about Him today. Make sure students don't put their names on these papers. Then collect them.

Stack the handouts in the front of the room and invite any students who want to come up, take one of the papers and pray for the need listed. You and your adult volunteers should pray for any papers that are left untaken. Make it clear that it is ultimately God's will that is done, not our own, so we're not trying to talk God into anything in our prayers, but rather confirm that we know that He can do anything.

Close in prayer, thanking Jesus that He can do *amazing* things in our lives.

All About Me

Take a few minutes to let us know all about you.

Name   Age

School   Grade

Number of brothers, sisters, stepbrothers or stepsisters

Color of your room

Favorite article of clothing

Favorite website

Your mom's middle name

What you get in trouble at home for the most

Vegetable you hate

Favorite television show

Things you like to do after school

Favorite dessert

What kind of work you'd like to do if you had to get a job in high school

© 1999 by Gospel Light. Permission to photocopy granted. *GP4U (God's Plan for You)*

Can It

Find someone who can do any of the following and have the person sign his or her initials in that square. If possible, have him or her demonstrate it for you.

I can burp my name.	I can bake chocolate chip cookies.	FREE	I can design my own web page	I can talk on the phone for three hours.	FREE
I can play a sport	FREE	I can water ski on one ski.	I can give you the number of my own private phone line.	I can understand all my math homework	I can sew my own clothes.
I can twirl a baton	I can tell you the capital of one of our neighboring states	FREE	I can hold my breath for 60 seconds.	FREE	I can tell you what day it is today.
FREE	I can do an "olly" on my skateboard.	I can tell you my favorite thing about our youth leader.	FREE	I can recite five phone numbers by heart (other than my own)	I can cut other people's hair.
I can play the flute	FREE	I can draw an elephant (you might need to prove this one!)	I can snap my fingers on both hands.	I can do a cartwheel.	FREE
I can rollerblade.	I can curl my tongue.	I can change a diaper.	FREE	I can keep my eyes open for 15 seconds without blinking	I can speak French.

© 1999 by Gospel Light. Permission to photocopy granted. *GP4U (God's Plan for You)*

Twin Stories

Check out John 5:1-9 and John 6:16-21. Write down what these verses have in common in the following areas:

1. What happens in both stories?

2. Who's involved in both stories?

3. What do both stories tell us about Jesus?

4. What other things do both stories have in common?

© 1999 by Gospel Light. Permission to photocopy granted. *GP4U (God's Plan for You)*

Jesus, You Can...

Take a few minutes to finish the sentence by writing down something that you know Jesus can do in your own life, given what you've learned about Him today.

JESUS, YOU CAN...

Take a few minutes to finish the sentence by writing down something that you know Jesus can do in your own life, given what you've learned about Him today.

Jesus, You can...

Take a few minutes to finish the sentence by writing down something that you know Jesus can do in your own life, given what you've learned about Him today.

Jesus, You can

SESSION 4

Jesus Paid the Price

Leader's Devotional

Recently, the Barna Research Group conducted a nationwide telephone survey of 600 American teenagers and discovered some important youth ministry trends.

THE GOOD NEWS

- Nearly one in three teenagers attends a youth group every week.
- The number one thing that teens like about their youth group is their relationships with their friends and their youth leader (just when you thought you weren't very significant in their lives).
- Seventy-two percent of youth group attendees say their faith is very important.
- Seventy percent of youth group attendees believe the Bible is totally accurate.
- Three out of four youth group attendees feel a responsibility to share their faith.

THE BAD NEWS

- Four out of five youth group attendees say there is no such thing as absolute truth.
- One out of six youth group attendees say there's no meaning or purpose in life.
- Fifty-five percent of youth group attendees demonstrate the identical moral behaviors as those who do not attend youth groups.
- Six out of 10 believe the Holy Spirit is just a symbol of God's presence.
- Half of youth group attendees are not born-again Christians.[1]

Reread that last bad news item for a moment: Half of youth group attendees are not born-again Christians. Actually, instead of falling into the "bad news" category, you might argue that it is partially "good news." Although half of students might not have asked Jesus to take over their lives yet, *you* have the chance to regularly be an evangelist—to share the good news of Jesus Christ with them.

In fact, you have the chance to do it during this session. Of the five sessions in this series, this session provides the clearest chance for students to decide who Jesus is and what name they would give Him in their own lives. As C.S. Lewis wisely taught decades ago, Jesus is either liar, lunatic or Lord. May the percentage of students who are born-again skyrocket as they realize that He is, indeed, Lord.

1. Research reported in *Teenagers Describe Their Church Youth Group: A Study of U.S. Teens, Ages 13 to 18*, by the Barna Research Group, Ltd., Ventura, CA, fall 1998.

Session 4 Jesus Paid the Price

Key Verse

"They found the stone rolled away from the tomb, but when they entered, they did not find the body of the Lord Jesus." Luke 24:2,3

Biblical Basis

Luke 22:66—24:35; 1 Peter 3:18

Focus of This Session

We can receive forgiveness for our sins and new life because of Jesus' death and resurrection.

Aims of This Session

During this session students will:
- Examine the historical facts surrounding Jesus' death and resurrection;
- Feel relieved that their sins can be wiped away;
- Act by deciding to ask Jesus to take over their lives.

Approach the Word

15 MINUTES

OBJECTIVE
To help students realize that life is a whole lot easier when they're not carrying extra loads.

MATERIALS AND PREPARATION NEEDED
❏ Twenty sheets of paper
❏ Two sturdy bedsheets (sturdy enough to absorb all the strength that a pubescent 13-year-old can muster!)
❏ Upbeat music

Ahead of time, make sure the room is cleared of extra furniture and have upbeat music playing as students arrive, creating a lively atmosphere.

Begin by greeting students and explaining that today you're going to see who is stronger and faster: Girls or guys. Send the girls along with 10 pieces of paper and one bedsheet to one side of the room, and the guys along with the other 10 pieces of paper and the other bedsheet to the other side of the room. Ask students to wad up the papers into individual balls (a task they're sure to enjoy, but just make sure they don't throw them at anyone yet; that will come later) as you select three pairs from each team. (**Note:** Be careful to pair up students who are of similar physical size.) One of each pair will be a "puller" and the other will be the "rider."

Explain the rules of the game: One pair at a time from each team will attempt to reach the other end of the room and back with the puller pulling the rider on the bedsheet. Here's the catch: The rest of each team will line up along their assigned side of the room and throw the wadded-up papers at the opposite team's puller. If the puller gets hit, he or she has to stop and the puller and rider have to switch places and the new puller resumes running. Throwers have to keep at least one foot against the wall in order to throw. (**Suggestion:** Have other adults watch the throwers to make sure they keep their feet against the wall.) If they throw and miss, *anyone* on either team can run and grab the piece of paper off the floor, return to their wall, and use it as ammunition. When a pair returns to the starting point, it's the next pair's turn to go. The winning team is the one who gets all three pairs across the room and back first.

Reminder:

Don't forget Memory Mania!

After you've declared the winning team, ask all of the students to sit down as you ask the pullers: **Was it tiring to pull the sheet? Would it have been easier if there was no one sitting on the sheet? Or better yet, if there was no sheet at all? How would you like to go through life burdened down with a heavy load?**

So far we've learned about how our sin separates us from God. Not only that, but it makes our lives harder, just like the sheet with the rider did in this game. Today we're going to look at how knowing Jesus will help us run free and wipe away things like sin that slow us down.

Bible Exploration One

 30 MINUTES

OBJECTIVE

To familiarize students with the historical account of Jesus' death and resurrection.

MATERIALS AND PREPARATION NEEDED
- Several Bibles
- Pens or pencils
- Copies of "Say What?" (p. 61)

Explain: **Last time we looked at Jesus' life and how amazing it was. Today we're going to look at Jesus' death and become detectives to try to figure out the details surrounding it. No other death has been like Jesus', so you're going to have to pay close attention to all of the details in Luke 22:66—24:12.** Ask students to take turns reading a few verses from Luke 22:66—24:12 until the passage is finished.

Divide students into groups of three and distribute Bibles (making sure each group has at least one Bible), copies of "Say What?" and pens or pencils. Instruct them to work through the handout as a group to figure out two things: First, who said each quote or statement, and second, the order the statements appear in Luke 22:66—24:12.

After 12 to 15 minutes, ask groups to volunteer to share their answers about who said what. The correct answers are: (A) Crowd, (B) Council of Elders, (C) Soldiers, (D) Jesus,

(E) Council of Elders, (F) Jesus, (G) Jesus, (H) Jesus, (I) Pilate, (J) Crowd, (K) Whole assembly, (L) Pilate, (M) Jesus, (N) Pilate, (O) Women at the tomb.

Next, discuss the order of the statements using questions such as: **What happened first? What happened next? Then what happened?** The correct order is B, E, H, K, I, N, L, O, A, J, F, M, C, G, D.

Ask students to vote on which statement of Jesus' was the most important, as well as which statement from anyone else was the most important. Make sure students understand that the only charge leveled against Jesus was that He was King of the Jews. Because Israel was under Roman rule, Jesus' claim to be King of the Jews threatened Roman sovereignty. Yet it was part of His fulfillment of Old Testament prophecies.

In addition, be sure to point out Jesus' pain as He cried out, "Father, into Your hands I commit my spirit." Explain: **His death—His painful death—was necessary so He could experience the pain of our sin and free us from its deathly consequences. That's because it wasn't Jesus' sin that caused His death, but ours. Since our sin was keeping us from God, He created a bridge from Him to us. Jesus' death on the cross for our sin and His coming to life after His death builds this bridge.**

Conclude by explaining: **This isn't just some story that someone made up. It's historical fact. No one has ever found Jesus' body. There are graves for Buddha, Mohammed and all the other religious leaders of the world, but no one ever found Jesus' body. The tomb was empty! Jesus' resurrection is at the heart of our Christian faith. In fact, the apostle Paul, who at first persecuted believers and then was converted by Jesus' appearance to him, said, in effect, that if Jesus didn't rise from the dead, then you might as well chuck the Christian faith. It wasn't just founded on feelings, but facts.**

> **Note:** If you are completing this session in one meeting, skip to "Conclusion and Decision."

> **Two-Meeting Track:** If you want to spread this session over two meetings, STOP here and close in prayer. Inform students of the content to be covered in your next meeting.

Review and Approach

 15 MINUTES

OBJECTIVE
To show students that heartburn can be a positive thing!

MATERIALS AND PREPARATION NEEDED
- Candy
- A blender
- Several small paper cups
- Paper towels
- A trash can lined with a plastic bag
- At least 15 different food items that can easily be blended in a blender (such as: bananas, yogurt, hot dogs, cheese spread, salsa, spaghetti sauce, tuna, mayonnaise, etc.)

Reminder:

Don't forget Memory Mania!

Welcome students and explain that you're going to begin with a game that is only for the strong of stomach. Divide students into two teams and ask for one volunteer from each team. Begin by putting three random ingredients into the blender; then add an additional ingredient into the blender (but don't blend it yet). The first volunteer gets to choose whether or not she wants to eat the four ingredients that have accumulated. If she does, she says "Blend," and the ingredients are blended together and poured into a cup. If she drinks it and doesn't spit it out into the nearby trash can, her team gets four million points, one million for each item. If she chooses not to drink it, she says, "Dare," at which point you add another item into the mixture and give the volunteer from the other team a chance to decide whether to blend or dare. If he chooses to drink the mixture, his team gets five million points, one million for each item. If he chooses to dare, a sixth item is added and the choice returns to the first volunteer. If both teams continue to dare until 10 items are in the blender, the person whose turn lands on the tenth item has to drink what's now in the blender. Every time the concoction is ingested, two new volunteers are selected and the game continues. Do this for four or five rounds, keeping track of points and awarding candy to the winning team.

This game will make you—and probably some of the students in the audience—nauseous and that is the point. Explain: **One of the things that causes our stomachs to hurt is heartburn. Has anyone here ever experienced heartburn** (surely someone who drank some of the disgusting concoction you just made is experiencing it right now!)? **Today we're going to look at one case when having heartburn was actually a good thing.**

Bible Exploration Two

30 MINUTES

OBJECTIVE

To help students understand how to recognize Jesus.

MATERIALS AND PREPARATION NEEDED
- Several Bibles
- Pens or pencils
- Blank paper
- A cassette answering machine (or cassette tape recorder)

Ahead of time, call four or five students and ask them to leave the identical one-sentence message on your answering machine, such as "I'll meet you on Monday." The callers should not say their names or any other additional information. Be sure to ask the students to call within the same 15-minute time frame so the messages will be consecutive. Ask them not to tell anyone what they've done, but to play along in ignorance during the session. Bring the answering machine to the session and you're ready to go.

> **Note:** This exercise won't work with a digital answering machine, unless it is equipped with a back-up battery so you don't lose the messages when you unplug it to bring to the meeting. If you don't have access to one of these or a cassette-style machine, substitute a cassette tape recorder instead and meet with the volunteers in person to have them record the message.

Ask students if they've ever heard a voice on an answering machine and thought it sounded familiar but couldn't quite place it. Explain that your problem is that this happened several times to you yesterday. Play the messages from your answering machine, distribute paper and pens or pencils. Instruct students to write down their guesses about the identity of these mystery callers. After a few minutes, replay the messages and ask the students who made the phone calls to identify themselves. Congratulate any students who guessed all five correctly.

Explain: **Although there were no answering machines in the Bible, people still had a hard time recognizing other people. Let's look at Luke 24:13-35.** Ask for volunteers to read the passage, and then discuss the following:

Why didn't Cleopas and his companion recognize Jesus? It had to be because of divine intervention.

How did the two describe Jesus? As a powerful prophet who was crucified and whose body is missing.

How did Jesus explain the truth about what happened? By using stories from the Old Testament.

When did Cleopas and the companion recognize who Jesus was? When He broke bread.

How did they describe how they felt when they walked with Jesus, even though they didn't know who He was? Their hearts were burning within them.

What does this mean? It means the encounter with Jesus totally affected their emotions and very being.

What did they do once they realized who Jesus was? They went back and told the other disciples who were gathered in Jerusalem.

Explain: **Jesus is with us all the time; we just don't always recognize Him. Can you think of a time in your own life when you knew Jesus was helping you or working in a situation that you were facing?** (You or one of your adult leaders may need to be ready to share a story as an example of what you're looking for.)

Discuss: **What keeps us from recognizing Jesus?** Our pride, our busyness, our focus on ourselves. **How can we be more ready to recognize who Jesus is, and how He might**

be working in and around us? Just like in the story, it's ultimately Jesus who shows us, but the more time we spend with Him in prayer and in studying about Him in the Bible, the easier it will be. If the two on the road hadn't been talking about Jesus, He might not have revealed Himself to them.

Conclusion and Decision

10 MINUTES

OBJECTIVE

To allow students to decide for themselves who Jesus is.

MATERIALS AND PREPARATION NEEDED

- ❑ Felt-tip pens
- ❑ Copies of "Name That Person" (p. 62), cut into individual cards
- ❑ Transparent tape
- ❑ Something that resembles a cross (i.e., a poster with a cross drawn on it or a cross made of two pieces of wood)
- ❑ **Option:** Copies of this session's memory verse, 1 Peter 3:18 on the "Memory Mania" handout (p. 23)

Explain: **The most important question you will ever have to answer is *Who is Jesus*? In Luke 23:38, the soldiers put a written notice that read, "This is the King of the Jews." What would you put if you could write a sign on Jesus' cross? What would you call Him?**

Continue: **We have a cross here. I'm going to give you a card and ask you to write how you would name Jesus. You may say "the guy who rose again" or "God's son who showed us what God was like" or maybe something simple like "Savior." It's up to you. Before I do, I'm going to read our memory verse, 1 Peter 3:18, because you might want to consider including it on your card: "For Christ died for sins once for all...to bring you to God."** Distribute felt-tip pens and a card from "Name That Person" to each student.

Have mellow worship music playing as students write on their cards. After a few minutes, ask students to come up and tape their cards to the cross.

Close in prayer by reading off some of the names from the cards that point to Jesus as Savior or risen Lord.

> **Note:** This is a great opportunity to ask any students who wrote the word "Savior" and understood for the first time tonight what it really means, to come see you right after the session so you can talk with them for a few minutes.

Say What?

Write the name of each person who said these quotes. (**Note:** Some of these aren't exact quotes, but descriptions of what the person might have said.)

A. Away with this man. Release Barabbas to us!

B. If you are the Christ, tell us.

C. Save yourself.

D. Father, into your hands I commit my spirit.

E. Are you then the Son of God?

F. Daughters of Jerusalem, do not weep for me.

G. Today you will be with me in paradise.

H. You are right in saying I am.

I. Are you the king of the Jews?

J. Crucify him! Crucify him!

K. We have found this man subverting our nation.

L. Herod, I'm glad you're my friend now.

M. Forgive them, for they do not know what they are doing.

N. I have found no basis for your charges against him.

O. Where did he go?

Now, list these sayings in the order that they appear in Luke.

Name That Person

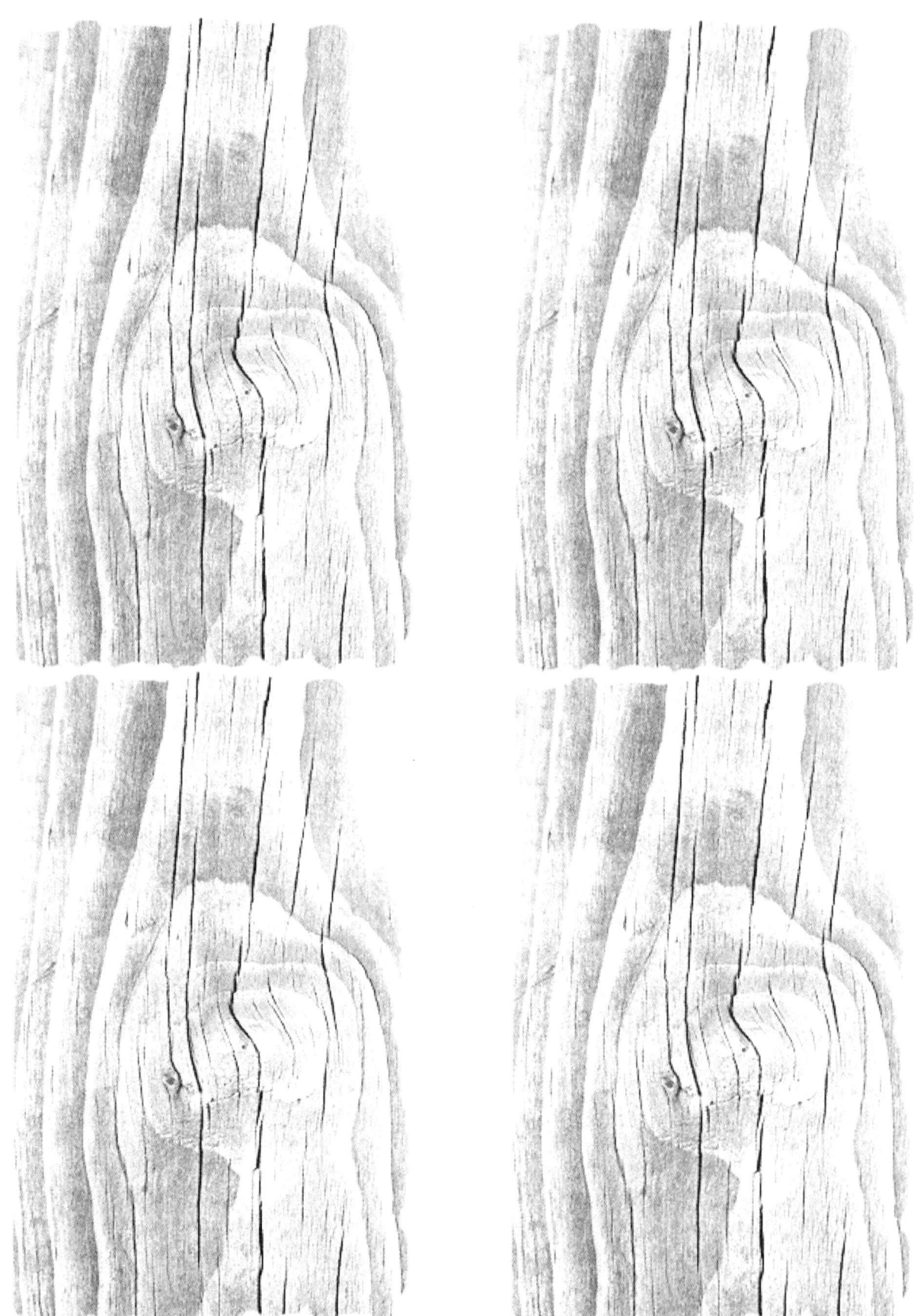

SESSION 5

Ambassadors for His Kingdom

Leader's Devotional

Imagine Jesus walking onto the junior high campus nearest your church. What would He see? What would He hear? What would other students say to Him during lunch? Even more interesting, what would He say back?

The mind-stretching truth is that Jesus *is* present on that junior high campus; that is, as long as it is attended by one or more Christian junior highers. When we give Jesus control of our lives, we become His ambassadors. He walks onto job sites, campuses—*everywhere*—with us. As His ambassadors we represent Him to others, both by how we live and what we say.

Most junior highers (and most adults for that matter) can't quite grasp this, so this session will give students some baby steps in learning how to be Christ's representative to their friends around them. It gives them suggestions for initial acts of love that they can show to others that are small in effort, but large in effect. It also gives them a clearer vision of bigger steps of love they can eventually take that will probably require them to make a more significant sacrifice of time, energy or maybe something even more costly, like their reputation or their desire to be popular.

We end this series with this session on being Christ's ambassadors because we want to give students the tools to live out the truths they've learned in the previous four sessions. Just as faith without works is dead, so truth without application remains paralyzed.

Session 5   Ambassadors for His Kingdom

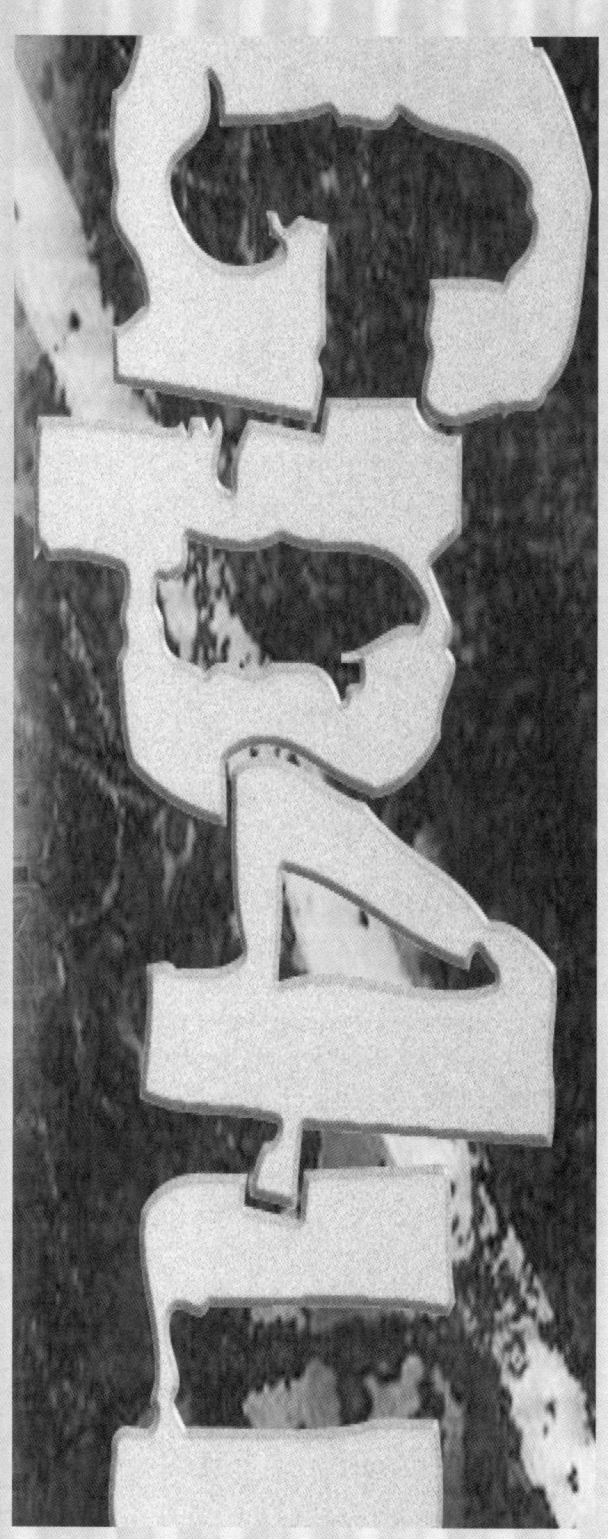

Key Verse

"But you will receive power when the Holy Spirit comes on you; and you will be my witnesses in Jerusalem, and in all Judea and Samaria, and to the ends of the earth." Acts 1:8

Biblical Basis

Acts 1:1-11; 2:42-47; 4:32-36; Ephesians 5:2

Focus of This Session

You can live as God's child and show His love to others.

Aims of This Session

During this session students will:
- Realize that the Holy Spirit is their new source of power;
- Be motivated to share the gospel with others through both their words and their actions;
- Act by choosing to show God's love to two people this week.

Approach the Word

 **15 MINUTES**

OBJECTIVE

To help students realize how hard it is to explain something when you can't figure out what to say.

MATERIALS AND PREPARATION NEEDED
- An overhead projector
- An overhead transparency copy of "Sound It Out" (p. 72)
- A blank piece of paper
- Candy prizes

Ahead of time, position the overhead projector so that it projects the "Sound It Out" image as large as possible on a screen or blank section of your front wall. Use the blank paper to cover the transparency and reveal only one phrase at a time.

Greet students and explain that you're going to start this session with a game that everyone can play. One at a time, you're going to reveal a series of phonetic sounds that combine to form a word or a phrase. Students should try to sound out the phrases, or they'll never figure out what the real phrase is. When a student thinks he knows the phrase, he should stand up and wait to be called on by you. Then he can share the phrase, and if he's right, receive a piece of candy. It's amusing, and sometimes downright hilarious, to see students making the phonetic sounds as they try to figure out the phrase. The correct answers are:
1. Santa Claus
2. Thomas Jefferson
3. Chiquita Banana
4. The Titanic
5. I love you
6. Christopher Columbus
7. Doctor Seuss
8. The Milky Way Galaxy
9. The Sound of Music
10. Bugs Bunny

After you've finished the game, congratulate everyone on how well they played. Discuss: **Don't you hate the feeling when you're trying to figure out what to say and you just**

Reminder:

Don't forget Memory Mania!

can't quite say it right? Have you ever had that kind of experience when you've tried to tell someone about church or your relationship with God?** You may want to share one of your own experiences at this point. Explain: **Thankfully, we don't have to rely on our own brains or our own mouths. God has given us a gift that makes it much easier to tell others about Him, and today we're going to unwrap that gift and find out what it means together.**

Bible Exploration One

 30 MINUTES

OBJECTIVE

To help students discover creative ways they can witness to others.

MATERIALS AND PREPARATION NEEDED
- Several Bibles
- An overhead projector
- An overhead transparency copy of "Sound It Out" (p. 72)
- Candy bars for prizes
- Three pieces of poster board
- Three (or six) different colored felt-tip pens
- Transparent tape

Ahead of time, tape the three pieces of poster board around the room and write one of the following words or phrases on each: "Jerusalem," "Judea/Samaria" and "Ends of the earth." **Note:** If your group is typically larger than 30 students, use six pieces of poster board instead of three, making sure to write the words or phrases each on two pages. You will also need six different colored felt-tip pens.

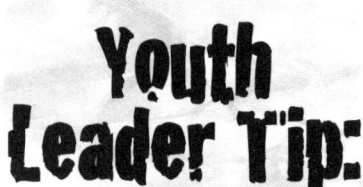

Youth Leader Tip:

Be prepared for students' questions in this exercise by reading Acts 1:1-11 several times!

Let students know that this is a chance for them to really stump you. Designate one of the students' Bibles as the "group Bible" and ask for different volunteers to read Acts 1:1-11 by passing the Bible around and reading one or two verses each.

After the passage has been read, put your own Bible away and distribute a Bible to anyone who doesn't have one already. Allow students five minutes to stump you with questions from the passage. They can ask anything that can be answered by Acts 1:1-11. Any student that stumps you will get a candy bar. This will be sure to cause students to pore over the passage with the reward of not only stumping you, but also getting a free candy bar!

After five minutes, explain that you have some questions for them; discuss:

What had happened to Jesus just before this event? He was killed, and then resurrected from the dead.

Why did Jesus want His followers to wait? He knew they weren't ready yet because they needed the power of His Holy Spirit.

What did the two men in white mean when they said Jesus was going to "come back"? Jesus is going to come back again to earth.

What are the differences between Jerusalem, Judea and Samaria and the rest of the earth? Jerusalem is the city the disciples were in while Jesus was talking with them. Judea referred to their own nation, while Samaria was a neighboring country. The ends of the earth includes everywhere else. To further illustrate these three locations, you may want to designate one or two students (or more, depending on how large your group is) in the center of your meeting room as Jerusalem, because it was right where the disciples were. You can call the students near them Judea and Samaria, while the rest of the students represent the far corners of the earth.

Point to the pieces of poster board hanging on the walls in the room. Divide students into three groups (or six groups, if your group is large enough) and give each group a different colored pen. Ask them to go to one of the posters and give them two or three minutes to write down any ideas they can think of to be witnesses in that area. After three minutes, stop them and ask each group to rotate to the next poster to the left and use their felt-tip pen to write down any ideas for the location written on the paper that the first group didn't already write. Repeat this rotation one more time so students have the chance to write additional ideas for the third location.

Read the answers aloud and comment on those that are most interesting or relevant to your group, as well as any that are particularly amusing. Explain: **There is no limit to the ways God can use us, which means we get to be creative and come up with both big and small ways we can show His love to our own Jerusalem, Judea, Samaria and the ends of the earth.**

> **Bible Bonus Note:**
>
> Interestingly, Jerusalem, Judea and Samaria form a virtual outline of Acts. Acts 1—7 describes the disciples witnessing in Jerusalem, Acts 8—9 tells about their work in Judea and Samaria and the rest of the book of Acts depicts their ministry to the ends of the earth, including Antioch, Asia Minor, Greece, Caesarea and Rome.

> **Note:** If you are completing this session in one meeting, skip to "Conclusion and Decision."

> **Two-Meeting Track:** If you want to spread this session over two meetings, STOP here and close in prayer. Inform students of the content to be covered in your next meeting.

Review and Approach

15 MINUTES

OBJECTIVE
To help students grasp that once they are Christians they're also members of God's family.

MATERIALS AND PREPARATION NEEDED
- Pens or pencils
- Copies of "Family Facts" (p. 73)
- Candy prize

Reminder: Don't forget Memory Mania!

Greet students and ask if any of them would like a chance to win some candy. Of course the answer will be yes (unless you have an abnormally health-conscious group of junior highers!). Distribute pens or pencils and copies of "Family Facts" and instruct students to answer the categories to figure out how many points they get for their own family. Give the candy prize to the student who received the most points.

Explain: **For some of us when we think of our families, we smile. For others when we think of our families, we frown. Some of us may not even know our families. Today we're going to talk about a family that we have. Any of us who have asked Jesus to be our Savior and**

Lord are now part of God's family, and as we'll see today, God's family takes care of its members.

Bible Exploration Two

30 MINUTES

OBJECTIVE

To help students experience how it feels to help someone in need, or maybe how it feels when you don't help someone in need.

MATERIALS AND PREPARATION NEEDED
- Copies of "Ancestors" (p. 74)
- Several 3x5-inch index cards
- Pens or pencils
- Three paper bags
- Cookies

Ahead of time, ask a friend who will not be known or recognized by students to dress like a "needy" person, looking for money and/or food. Also, place the cookies inside one of the paper bags.

Hold up the paper bag with the cookies and explain that you have good news: you brought just enough cookies for everyone to have one. At this point, your "needy" friend should walk into your meeting room. Although you continue to talk about how glad you are that the group isn't much bigger or you'd be short of cookies, the needy person should get the attention of students by looking around the room, maybe smelling some random things around the room, possibly muttering under his breath, burping—whatever it takes to remind students that there is someone in their room who doesn't usually show up there. The needy person should come to the front of the room and ask if you have any food or money to help him out. Explain that you're not comfortable giving him money and that, although you have some food for students, there's not enough for him.

At this point, you'll have to play it by ear depending on how students respond. If they urge you to give him the cookies, go ahead and do so. If they don't do anything and look at you for cues in how to respond (which is the most likely possibility), let the needy person know that he will have to look elsewhere for food.

Once the needy person leaves, discuss the following, choosing those that are most pertinent to your group's response:

What did you think when you saw the needy person?
How many of you wished he would just leave?
Why did you want to give (or not give) him the food?
How did you feel about how I responded to him?
How do you think God would want us to respond if this happens again?

Explain that Acts 2:41-47 and Acts 4:32-37 give the answers to the last question. Distribute a pen or pencil and a copy of "My Ancestors" and explain: **The Bible is full of your ancestors, not necessarily your biological ancestors, but at least your spiritual ancestors. I want everyone on the left side of the room to underline anything that describes *what* your ancestors did. Everyone on the right should underline anything that describes the *results* of what your ancestors did.**

After four or five minutes, ask volunteers to share one item at a time that they underlined. Ask a few student volunteers to write down these items on separate index cards, placing those that come from the students on the left side of the room in one bag, and those that come from the students on the right side of the room in another bag. When students have shared all of their underlined items, pull one index card out of the bag describing what the ancestors did, and ask students to come up with two ways they could do that this week. Repeat with several index cards. Conclude by asking: **If you could go back and treat the needy person who came to our room today differently, what would you do? If you could summarize what we learned in one word, what would it be?** The most obvious answer is "giving," but make sure you drive that point home yourself if students don't.

Conclusion and Decision

15 MINUTES

OBJECTIVE

To help students choose two people they can serve this week.

Materials and Preparation Needed
- ❑ Pens or pencils
- ❑ Copies of "Circle Up" (p. 75)
- ❑ **Option:** Copies of this session's memory verse, Ephesians 5:2 on the "Memory Mania" handout (p. 23)

Explain: **We're going to finish this session by thinking about people around us who might need help, in our own Jerusalem, Judea, Samaria and ends of the earth.** Distribute pens or pencils and copies of "Circle Up" as you continue: **On this sheet, write the names of your family or close friends in the innermost circle. In the next circle, write the names of people you don't know as well, like neighbors or other students at school. In the outside circle, write the names of people or groups of people who live even farther away.**

Allow students seven or eight minutes to write the names; then ask them to choose two names from their papers. Instruct them to write at the bottom of their pages one need for each of these two people that they could realistically meet this week. A need might be to hear about Jesus or it might be a physical need, such as helping with homework or talking to someone during lunch.

Explain: **Now that we have the power of the Holy Spirit, God can use us to give to others and meet their needs. Our memory verse for this session is Ephesians 5:2, in which Paul summarized everything we have talked about today: "And live a life of love, just as Christ loved us and gave himself up for us as a fragrant offering and sacrifice to God." How does living a life of love make us a fragrant offering to God, too?**

Close in prayer, thanking God that knowing Him as Savior makes us part of His new family, and asking Him to give us strength to meet the needs of these two people.

Sound It Out

Solve these puzzles by saying them out loud, over and over, fast and faster, repeating the phrase, until you "hear" the answer. Example: LAW SAND JEALOUS (place) is Los Angeles.

1. SAND TACKLE LAWS (fictional character)

2. TALL MISS CHEF HER SUN (person)

3. CHICK HE TUB AN AN US (product)

4. THOUGH TIGHT AN HICK (thing)

5. AISLE OH VIEW (phrase)

6. CARESS TROUGHER CLUMP US (person)

7. DOCKED HEARSE WHOSE (person)

8. THUMB ILL KEY WAKE OWL LICKS HE (place)

9. THESE HOUND DOVE MOO SICK (movie)

10. BUCKS SPUN HE (fictional character)

Family Facts

Figure out how many points you would have for your family from the following questions:

Give yourself...

_____ 10 points for each family member you live with.

_____ 29 points for each family member you've talked with today.

_____ 21 points for each family member in your home who works at a paying job.

_____ 40 points for something you've done this week to help someone in your family.

_____ 72 points if you have a picture of someone in your family with you.

_____ 28 points if you have a picture of someone in your family hanging up in your room.

_____ 37 points for every stepparent or stepbrother or stepsister you have.

_____ 22 points for every vowel in your last name.

_____ 30 points if your last name is less than four letters.

_____ 17 points for every birthday of a family member you know by heart.

_____ 43 points if you have something with you that belongs to someone else in your family.

_____ 7 points for every job you can name that your grandparents ever had.

_____ 57 points if you can name what the parent(s) you live with do at work.

_____ 36 points if you share a room with someone else in your family.

_____ 18 points for each nephew or niece you have (which means you are already an aunt or an uncle).

_____ 77 points if you are the only one from your family at church today.

_____ 63 points if you haven't fought with anyone in your family in the last 48 hours (including fights over chores, computer use, television programs or homework).

_____ 48 points if you said "I'm sorry" to a family member this week.

_____ 7 points for every cousin you've seen in the last 12 months.

_____ 45 points if you were adopted.

_____ YOUR TOTAL POINTS

Ancestors

Acts 2:41-47

They committed themselves to the teaching of the apostles, the life together, the common meal, and the prayers. Everyone around was in awe—all those wonders and signs done through the apostles! And all the believers lived in a wonderful harmony, holding everything in common. They sold whatever they owned and pooled their resources so that each person's need was met.

They followed a daily discipline of worship in the Temple followed by meals at home, every meal a celebration, exuberant and joyful, as they praised God. People in general liked what they saw. Every day their number grew as God added those who were saved.

Acts 4:32-37

The whole congregation of believers was united as one—one heart, one mind! They didn't even claim ownership of their own possessions. No one said, "That's mine; you can't have it." They shared everything. The apostles gave powerful witness to the resurrection of the Master Jesus, and grace was on all of them.

And so it turned out that not a person among them was needy. Those who owned fields or houses sold them and brought the price of the sale to the apostles and made an offering of it. The apostles then distributed it according to each person's need.

Joseph, called by the apostles "Barnabas" (which means "Son of Comfort"), a Levite born in Cyprus, sold a field that he owned, brought the money and made an offering of it to the apostles.

From THE MESSAGE[1]

Note:
1. Scripture taken from *THE MESSAGE*. Copyright © by Eugene H. Peterson, 1993, 1994, 1995. Used by permission of NavPress Publishing Group.

Circle Up

Take a few minutes and write as many names as you can think of that fit in these three circles. The inner circle is "Jerusalem," meaning your family and close friends. The middle circle is "Judea and Samaria," meaning neighbors and students that you see often but don't know as well. The outer circle is "the rest of the world," meaning anyone else you can think of, ranging from the president of the United States to the people who live in Slovenia (yup, that's a real country in Europe!).

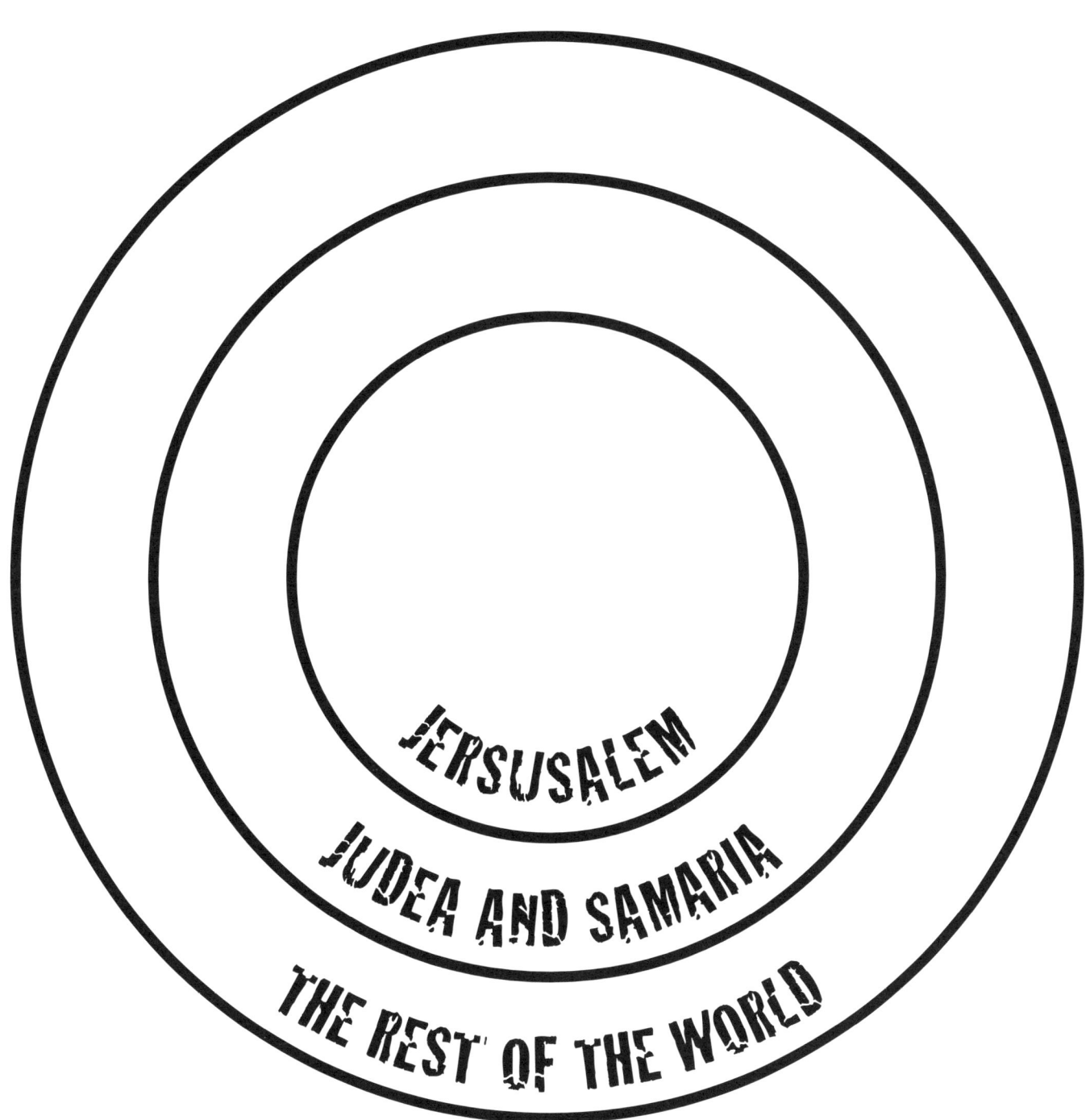

How can I get to know Jesus?

GOD'S LOVE for us is so great that He wants us to get to know Him. We can always count on His love because God *is* love.

> And so we know and rely on the love God has for us. God is love (1 John 4:16).

OUR SIN is what separates us from God. We sin anytime we fall short of God's plan for us, which means we sin every day. Our sin separates us from God not only in this life, but also when we die. Without God's plan to rescue us, none of us would have any hope of feeling His love and His relief from our pain right now or once we die.

> For all have sinned and fall short of the glory of God (Romans 3:23).

GOD'S PLAN of salvation is the cross of Jesus Christ. God sent His Son, Jesus, to die in our place so that we could be rescued from our sins, experience true life right now on earth and live with Him in heaven once we die. Jesus is the only way to be saved from the sin that separates us from God. Jesus said,

> "I am the way and the truth and the life. No one comes to the Father except through me" (John 14:6).

OUR CHOICE to accept God's plan is all we need to do to receive the gift of salvation that rescues us from our sins. God offers this salvation, but He never forces us to accept Him; it's our choice either to ask God's Son to take over our life or to reject Him.

> For God so loved the world that he gave his one and only Son, that whoever believes in him shall not perish but have eternal life (John 3:16).

Would you like to make the choice to ask Jesus to take over your life right now?

Jesus loves you so much that you can get to know Him by praying and asking Him to take over your life. You can use your own words or follow this prayer:

> Jesus, I believe You are the Son of God and that You died on the cross for my sins. Forgive me of my sins and be the Lord of my life. Thank You for dying for me and making it possible for me to live with You in heaven forever. Amen.

© 1999 by Gospel Light. Permission to photocopy granted. *GP4U (God's Plan for You)*

How Can I Get to Know Jesus?

Big Word #1: Love

"And so we know and rely on the love God has for us. God is love. Whoever lives in love lives in God, and God in him." 1 John 4:16

Big Word #2: Sin

"For all have sinned and fall short of the glory of God." Romans 3:23

Big Word #3: Jesus

"Jesus answered, 'I am the way and the truth and the life. No one comes to the Father except through me.'" John 14:6

Big Word #4: Choose

"For God so loved the world that he gave his one and only Son, that whoever believes in him shall not perish but have eternal life." John 3:16

© 1999 by Gospel Light. Permission to photocopy granted. *GP4U (God's Plan for You)*